HOLMFIRTH
THE STORY OF TL   IN HOLMFIRTH

Ian Harlow

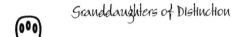
This book is dedicated to

Aimee Rebecca Gladish

And   Lucy Danielle Gladish

Granddaughters of Distinction

Alistair Lofthouse
DESIGN &
PRINT

Designed by Alistair Lofthouse
Printed and published by:
ALD Design & Print
279 Sharrow Vale Road
Sheffield S11 8ZF

Telephone 0114 267 9402
E:mail a.lofthouse@btinternet.com

ISBN 1-901587-48-7

First published August 2004

See Also:
The Dramatic Story of The Sheffield Flood   Peter Machan   ISBN 1-901587-05-3

ACKNOWLEDGEMENTS

Much of the material concerning the recollections of the Great Flood of 1852 are contained in the booklet 'The Holmfirth Flood caused by the bursting of the Bilberry Reservoir on Thursday morning, February 5th, 1852'. This was published in 1910 (58 years after the event) and republished in 1991 in a limited edition. I have also referred to a small handbook 'On the Trail of the Holmfirth Flood, 1852' by Gordon and Enid Minter, which contains much interesting material for the visitor wishing to visit the scenes described in this book..

I am grateful to Mr Brian Haigh and Mr John Rumsby of Kirklees Community History Service for all their efforts to locate the illustrations of the Great Flood, derived from very old photographs and lithographs of the scenes. I thank the staff at the Holmfirth Postcard Museum, in addition to the many individuals whose memories are used in this narrative.

The Holmfirth Flood of 1944 affected everyone living in the town and the surrounding areas. Some individual flood memories have been collected, on tape and in writing, by the Holme Valley Civic Society - Local History Group, and I am indebted to Mr Frank Burley (now deceased) for the chance to see and quote from some of these records.

I am grateful to Mr Trevor Bray for the use of the photographs which illustrate the story of the 1944 Holmfirth Flood. It was Mr Bray's father who utilised some of his precious photographic materials (strictly rationed during wartime, even for professional photographers) to make virtually the only pictorial record of these events. By a curious coincidence the notice of wartime security also contains an advertisement for Mr Bray's father at the Ribbleden Studios. It should be noted that the telephone number in use is still the same, over 50 years on, with the addition of a few leading digits.

Finally, I should like to thank my granddaughter, Lucy Gladish for using her artistic talents in the sketch maps of the Holme Valley

HOLMFIRTH FLOODS
THE STORY OF THE FLOODS IN HOLMFIRTH

INDEX OF CHAPTERS

CHAPTER 1

PORTRAIT OF THE HOLME VALLEY

The Holme Valley has been subjected to flash floods on several occasions over the centuries. Before the industrial revolution and the building of the factories (or Mills, as they are called locally) in the second half of the eighteenth century, most of these floods would be inconvenient but not disastrous. The population lived and worked on the farms and cottage industries higher up the slopes and a flooded river would cause extra maintenance work with perhaps the rebuilding of some banks and bridges.

The mills, however, had to be built as near to the riverside as possible. The river would provide power through watermills to run the machines and also be available to wash, scour and dye the wool. All down the valley each mill would divert water into a mill dam and return used and surplus water. With luck the flow of water would be sufficient for each mill to have a good supply of fresh water, not too polluted by the waste of mills higher up the valley. Even the occasional flash flood could be useful to flush away waste for the benefit of everybody. Excess water would clean out all the debris arising both from the mills and from the households along the riverside.

Many of these mill dams or reservoirs have been converted to alternative uses. The old mill races have disappeared, but the old reservoirs are recognisable even when they are silted up, overgrown or even built over.

The expansion of the mills required workers and their dwellings were built lower down the slopes and nearer the river. These cottages were not only near to the mills (useful, in that the workers did not need to waste energy on travelling too far); they were also built on the steeper slopes that were not suitable for productive farming.

Many of these houses still exist; being built of solid stone they are almost as indestructible as the mountains themselves. Many are built as four or five storey structures, with the lower house (the underdwelling) opening out just above the river bank and a second house approached higher up the slope facing away from the river. The upper dwelling would be considered a superior property, since it would have extra height, sometimes sufficient for a small attic or garret room. Some even have a third dwelling in between the upper and lower premises approached from the side. It all depended on the steepness of the slope and the lie of the land.

This architectural feature can lead to some unusual situations. At least one house, quite small and in the middle of a row of similar houses, has three different addresses, including two different Post Codes. Other cottages, built on slopes or hemmed in by other properties, would be constructed to take full advantage of the space available. The result is that some houses have unusual shape and rare character - 'period charm', the estate agents would call it. Naturally, no consideration was given to space for vehicles of any kind and modern inhabitants can find parking extremely awkward.

Living conditions in these cottages were very restrictive. When originally built they would have one room downstairs with stone flagstones over bare earth and perhaps a separate scullery or pantry area, with a flight of stone stairs up to the next floor. The first floor, normally the sleeping floor, would be an open space, without partitions to give a measure of privacy. For those with an attic or garret, entry would normally be by means of a ladder from the first floor. Inhabitants would need to be athletic and immodest, given the way in which families had to live so closely together.

Being built into the hillsides, many properties would be prone to chronic dampness. Even so, there would be no bathroom and even a cold water tap was an unusual luxury; one tap, if it existed, would normally be shared by a group of cottages. Otherwise they would need a stream or one of the stone wells fed from springs which still exist on many hillsides in the area. Earth toilets would be built at a distance from the houses, one privy serving several families. They would be cleaned out regularly, a most unenviable task. Frequently cottages contained weaving equipment on the upper floors, to take advantage of as much daylight as possible for working the looms. These cottage industries continued to flourish, even when mills had been built to produce fine cloth in quantity with all the modern machinery.

The custom of the Victorians to have large families meant that space inside the houses could be very limited. A family with six or eight children was not uncommon, so we can imagine the conditions under which they lived. Rooms would be scantily furnished and household chattels limited. Carpets would be very rare, although some would have small mats to keep out the cold and damp from the stone flagged floor. Frequently straw was used to keep the cottage a little cosier and this would be replaced as required. It was often necessary to sleep three or four children to a bed.

Food would be kept and prepared in the scullery or pantry, but cooking would be done in an open range in the main downstairs room. This would be known as the living room and that describes it exactly. It would serve as a kitchen, a dining room and a sitting room (lounges had not been invented); some might call it a parlour. The open fire would roast the dinner (everything in one oven), bake the bread, prepare fry-ups, boil the kettle and allow all members of the family to make their own toast. In winter, with ill fitting doors and windows, the fire would be the main comfort feature of the house.

Very few of the cottages would be owner occupied. Most would belong to a rich landowner (frequently the mill owner) and rent would be charged. If a man lost his job, he would probably lose his house as well, unless he could somehow afford to continue paying the rent. Movement between houses would occur as a man's fortune varied; if he was promoted, he would move up the social scale by renting a more imposing property. If he was ill or injured, a movement down the social scale was a likely result. If a family was so destitute that it could not afford to pay the rent, it would arrange to disappear in a 'moonlight flit'.

All this construction was vulnerable to the occasional flash floods which are described in this book. The cramped conditions in the cottages meant that they could easily become deathtraps. The understanding of safety from fire and flood was not a big consideration for the Victorian cottage or mill builders; nor, as we shall see, for builders of reservoirs.

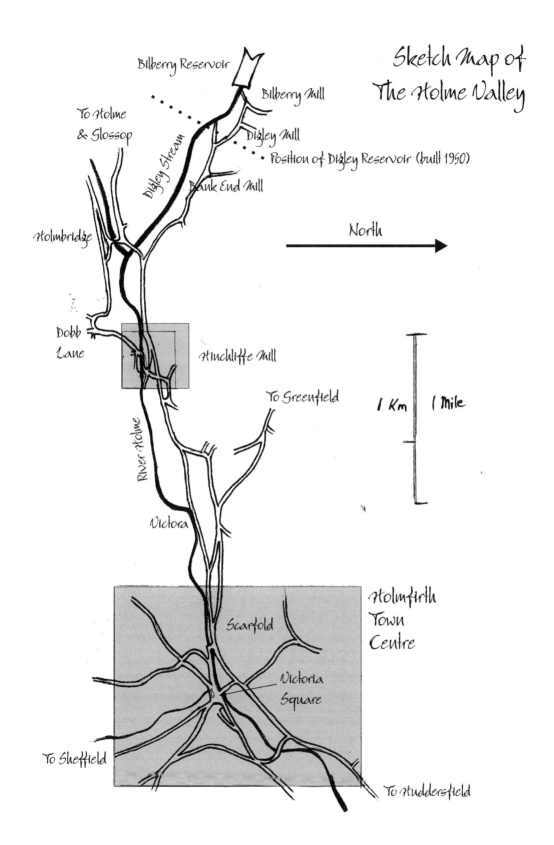

Sketch Map of
The Holme Valley

Bilberry Reservoir

Bilberry Mill

To Holme
& Glossop

Digley Mill

Position of Digley Reservoir (built 1950)

Digley Stream

Bank End Mill

Holmbridge

North

Dobb
Lane

Hinchliffe Mill

To Greenfield

1 Km   1 Mile

River Holme

Victora

Scarfold

Holmfirth
Town
Centre

Victoria
Square

To Sheffield

To Huddersfield

The working lives of most of the inhabitants of the Valley were governed by their location; they would work on either the farms or in one of the mills. A few enterprising characters would try to make their fortune by opening a shop, but their wealth creating opportunities would still be limited by the prosperity of their potential customers. Only the exceptionally gifted or exceptionally adventurous would be able to break free from the general pattern of life - if they were lucky and retained a fair measure of good health. Some of the wealthier middle classes, such as the mill owners and their families, would find it easier to get a good education and to see something of the world beyond the Holme Valley.

After working hours there was little time or opportunity for outside pursuits. Nevertheless other activities developed and these interests shaped the lives of the Valley inhabitants and still do today although to a more limited extent. The main outside collective interest was the Chapel (and sometimes the Parish Church if men wished to impress their employers). This provided opportunities for all kinds of social activity involving all the family; fellowships, discussion and interest groups for the men and women and Sunday Schools for the children. The Sunday Schools, before the passing of the Education Acts, provided the only chance for most children to learn to read and write as well as hearing stories from the Bible. In addition the men (mainly) developed interests in the game of cricket and in music, especially in brass bands and choirs or 'choral societies'. The valley supported many brass bands which competed with each other to provide great interest and rivalry.

The valley contained many small settlements, some near the river, but with a peppering of hillside villages. Each group of houses would adopt the name of the main residence, usually the farmer's house. This name has stuck, even when the original owner has been long forgotten. There would be no need for the houses to have numbers, until the time when the Post Office wished to identify houses more precisely. Most of the street names were derived from geographical features - Back Lane, Top Road, Crag End Bottom.

The houses were built as and when required, without benefit of town planning, which can give a group of properties a higgledy-piggledy charm. Old cottages mingle with very old houses and have aged and mellowed together. One indication of age can be inferred from the size of the windows; older cottages generally are smaller in height and have smaller windows. Another indication is provided by the blackening of the stone that has taken place. The old mill chimneys belched out thick black smoke over all the valley properties and left their sooty deposits everywhere.

All the enduring buildings in the valley were built of Yorkshire stone and in consequence there are many small quarries scattered around the area. These would generally be worked to provide just sufficient stone to build the small number of cottages nearby. These quarries would be normally opened up higher than the building work, so that stone could be easily be moved downhill to the site. Larger quarries would be opened to provide the materials to build the mills. The presence of these quarries and old buildings is often revealed by an odd 'lumpiness' in the ground, even though they are frequently so overgrown that they appear to be part of the historic landscape.

The extensive use of stone for building provides a potted history of the area, with an indication of the wealth of the inhabitants. Although stone buildings weather, this does little to disguise alterations and improvements that have been made. Windows and doors blocked in, outbuildings removed or rebuilt, extensions created and even new stories added to the houses will all leave their marks on buildings today, many years after the changes have taken place. Some builders have, very helpfully, incorporated a date on their work and a few have added initials, presumably indicating the first owner of the property.

The old and the new are sometimes revealed in the spelling of place names. In 1852 Holmbridge was spelt as Holmebridge; the omission of the 'e' is an understandable progression. Similarly Upper Bridge can also (and more properly, according to the local inhabitants) be written as one word Upperbridge. Written reports record both spellings, apparently indiscriminately. In 1852 Ford Gate in Hinchliffe Mill was named Fold Gate, even in a booklet printed in 1910. Both names could be used with justification, but the change of meaning seems odd.

Hinchliffe Mill has been variously spelt as Hinchey Mill (very old but still occasionally used colloquially) or Hinchcliffe Mill (even on Ordnance Survey maps). Local and official opinion calls it Hinchliffe Mill (omitting the second 'c'), so that it was with some embarrassment that a stone memorial recently opened on Victoria Bridge, right in the centre of Holmfirth, contains the spelling 'Hinchcliffe', carved in stone for all the world to see.

The quality of the stonework provides a useful guide to the prosperity of the owner. The finest houses would be taller and more imposing and built of smoothly sawn stone, evenly shaped and laid with inca-like precision. Frequently they would have carved door or window frames to proclaim the importance of the house and its inhabitants. The less wealthy would have stone of regular shape, but rough hewn on the outside. The cottages for the poorer members of the community would be built of stone of variable and uneven size. The walls of the houses and cottages would be thick, which had the advantage of being cool in summer and warm and cosy in winter; it is also long lasting. Even property over 300 years old still has a quality of solidity and stability today.

The abundance of stone from the quarries provides another characteristic feature of the area - dry stone walls built to separate fields. These tend to be many years old, and often extend far up into the hills. One can only wonder at the time and effort required to build something even as simple as a low stone wall. Each stone, which is very heavy, had to be carried on to the site, even up a steep mountain side, and carefully placed to provide a solid and long lasting construction, without cement. They were built with quality and skill, which is reflected in the fact that so many are still standing, even though they now show signs of age and vandalism.

The original pack horse track up the Holme Valley from Huddersfield to Holmfirth and into the Pennines meanders across the hills, linking all the small village communities, hamlets and farmsteads. Towards the end of the eighteenth century an improved new road was build, joining together all the mills. This took a more direct route, keeping

Sketch Map of Hinchliffe Mill

Dobb Lane

River Holme

To Holme

Stubbin Lane

Spring Lane

Mill Pond

Sol Gate (iron foot Gate)

Old Road

Woodhead Road

6 destroyed cottages, 1852

Hinchliffe Mill

Water Road

To Holmfirth

closer the river on the valley floor where all the mills were established. On its way it bye-passed the substantial centre of Honley and created a new centre for Holmfirth; it is now the main road down the Valley.

The old track and the new road intersect at many points, as a glance at the map will quickly reveal. One such place is in the centre of Holmfirth, where Victoria Street links the new road (Huddersfield Road) with the old valley track at what is now Victoria Square and bridge. The old road down the valley is joined at Holmfirth with a road over the hills from Sheffield. The road runs alongside the river for 200 yards (about 180 metres) at Hollowgate before swinging right over the river at Scarfold, then left, past the Tollhouse on its way over the Pennines towards either Greenfield or Glossop.

The River Holme is only eight miles or so in length from where it rises in a hundred small rivulets on Holme Moss and the nearby mountains until it joins the River Calder in Huddersfield. It flows in its early stages through deep ravines cut into the hillsides. These ravines were well wooded until the mills were built, but many of the trees were removed to make way for the new buildings and trackways up the valley. Since the floods and the closure of the mills the trees have re-established themselves to give the valley something like its original character.

The river flows at the start from west to east, falling over 300 feet (about 100 metres) before it swings north near Holmfirth, which is the main town in the valley. It is only a small place, hardly more than a village itself, except that the presence of a regular market entitles Holmfirth to call itself a town. As such it contains most of the civic buildings, and, at the time of the 1944 flood, was the headquarters of the Holmfirth Urban District Council.

There have been previous floods in the valley, whenever rainfall was exceptionally prolonged and heavy. In the last 300 years several floods were recorded, prior to the Great Flood of 1852.

On Sunday, 7th May, 1738, a cloud burst over Scholes Moor caused torrents to flow into Holmfirth down the valley of the Ribble River. The flood water forced its way into the Chapel of Holmfirth during morning service, causing great consternation and much damage, but there was no loss of life.

A more serious flood occurred in the afternoon of 23rd July, 1777, when a thunderstorm swelled the level of the river Holme and swept through the centre of Holmfirth. The enormous force washed away bridges, mills and houses and broke open some graves in the Parish Church burial ground. At Mill Hill, in the centre of the town, three men were carried away, directly in view of 'hundreds' of horrified spectators. The force of the water carried one of the bodies as far away as Horbury, near Wakefield. At the time this was known as The Great Flood until 1852.

On 21st September, 1821, at 7 o' clock in the evening a heavy rainstorm above Blacksyke caused a flood through Burnlee, causing much damage but no deaths.

There is little evidence of these floods now, as they have been dwarfed by the damage

Sketch Map of Holmfirth Town Centre

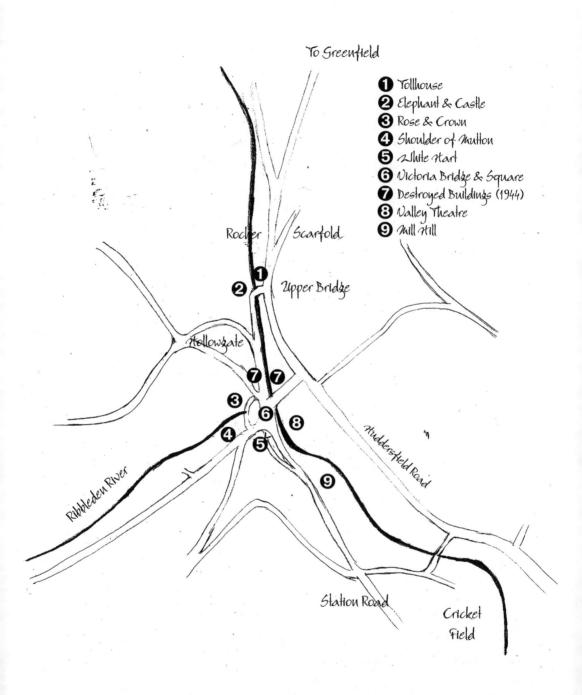

To Greenfield

1 Tollhouse
2 Elephant & Castle
3 Rose & Crown
4 Shoulder of Mutton
5 White Hart
6 Victoria Bridge & Square
7 Destroyed Buildings (1944)
8 Valley Theatre
9 Mill Hill

Rocher   Scarfold

Upper Bridge

Hollowgate

Ribbleden River

Huddersfield Road

Station Road   Cricket Field

caused by the 1852 and 1944 floods. The more recent inundations have their permanent memorials. Mr Quarmby's butcher's shop, near the river on Victoria Street, has a stone engraved with the height of the 1852 flood, some six feet from the ground. Although the shop has changed hands, Mr Quarmby has ensured that his name will not be forgotten, as it is molded into tiles embedded on the front of the shop.

A stone pillar, known affectionately as 'Owd Gen' (the Old Genn, in English) stands in Towngate, opposite the White Hart Inn, to record the Peace of Amiens. This was a break in hostilities in the Napoleonic war with France and its importance to the citizens of Holmfirth lay in the fact that the prosperity of the town depended so much on the trade in wool. This peace would, it was hoped, bring back their prosperity. It was a short lived hope. It is a sad irony that the town of Amiens, in Northern France, is built on the River Somme. Just 113 years after the Peace, thousands of British troops, including some from Holmfirth, were slaughtered in the Somme valley during the First World War.

The plaque on the pillar reads:

> This stone was erected in 1801 to commemorate the short Peace called the Peace of Amiens.

And a line indicates

> The height of the flood caused by the bursting of the Bilberry Reservoir on February 5th, 1852, whereby 81 lives were lost.

The height of the 1944 flood is not recorded on this pillar. However, the height of the floodwaters used to be recorded on a plaque attached to the Elephant and Castle public house at the Scarfold end of Hollowgate, until it was removed by a souvenir hunter. Near the bar inside the pub there is a small brass plate, regularly and lovingly polished, showing the height of the Whit Monday Flood.

The stories of the floods, as recorded in these pages, have been well documented over the years. The 1852 Flood, the Great Flood, was an early Victorian tragedy, although eclipsed in numbers by the Sheffield flood of 1864, when 250 people lost their lives. The 1944 Flood has been called the Forgotten Flood, because it occurred a few days before the Allied Invasion of Normandy. In consequence news was suppressed or muted for 10 days by wartime censorship restrictions; by the time details of the event were published the people in the country away from the Holme Valley had far weightier things to worry about.

On the wall of the bridge on Victoria Street is another, more detailed record covering both floods, so that they will be constantly remembered.

A more subtle record of the floods can be noted in the stonework, especially beside the river. Repairs on the stone walls of the buildings will show that work has been carried out: there will be evidence of filled-in windows and old roof edges traceable on tall side walls. Stone walls will reveal differences of construction in size, shape, colour, texture and skill of building. Stone does not easily weather to match.

After the ravages of the 1852 flood, work was put in hand which, it was thought, would make a similar flood impossible. Bilberry Reservoir, which burst its banks to cause the disaster, was reconstructed on a smaller scale. Work was planned by Huddersfield Corporation to build another reservoir downstream from Bilberry; this was intended, amongst other things, to provide a better control over the flow of the river. These plans were postponed because of the outbreak of war and in the event the 1944 flood occurred before the new dam was built.

THE GREAT FLOOD OF 1852

CHAPTER 2

CONSTRUCTION OF BILBERRY RESERVOIR - 1840

The first half of the nineteenth century saw enormous changes in English society, as the old rural ways of life were transformed in the Industrial Revolution. These changes affected all inhabitants and all occupations; in towns and in the country; on land and at sea; at home and abroad. In 1799, the old wooden ships at sea had changed little in design since Elizabethan times; Drake would have felt at home on Nelson's ships. Fifty years later all these had been consigned to history and metal ships were being built.

Within the country many people were disappearing from rural areas into the rapidly developing industrial towns. Canals were being built at the beginning of the period; they were being superseded by railways by the middle of the century. Both these methods of communications, for goods and for people, required much investment and upheaval for communities affected. Ground had to be leveled and strengthened, cuttings made through (sometimes) solid rock, embankments created and bridges built. A few tunnels were being bored where all other methods failed. All this work was being carried out to service the new mills and factories which were springing up all over the country.

The Holme Valley had its share of mills to process the wool of the local sheep to make fine worsted cloth, exported all over the world. It was said that the uniforms of Napoleon's armies were made from Huddersfield cloth. As noted in the last chapter, the citizens of Holmfirth erected a memorial column in the town to celebrate the Peace of Amiens, negotiated with the French Emperor in 1801. The peace only lasted six months, but the column still stands on Towngate, alongside the public toilets.

All the machinery in the Valley was powered by water mills, to take advantage of the flow of the River Holme. Each mill had its own mill race, which was built alongside the river to turn a huge waterwheel, which in turn set the looms in motion. Most mills created their own mill ponds by diverting water from the main stream and using the extra weight gained to keep a more constant flow, especially in the dryer months. The water in the river could be used time and time again by each successive mill in the valley; in theory it was very efficient and economical.

There were two difficulties in practice. One of these was pollution, in that local inhabitants would throw all kinds of debris into the river, as they had done for centuries. This could clog up the flow of water and limit its effectiveness to power the water wheels and to wash and dye wool. The second problem was that during dry spells (and even the Holme Valley would enjoy these from time to time) water flow would drop so low that it was inadequate to turn the millwheels. Local action could be taken to help with the pollution, but the lack of water in some summers required a more considered approach.

The solution to the problem lay in controlling the flow of water. During the winter and in other periods of heavy rain, water would need to be held in the mountains and allowed to flow at a regular and measured rate throughout the year. The extremes of weather would therefore by modified for the benefit of all the people in the valley. With this in mind the mill owners sponsored an Act of Parliament to build the dams (or reservoirs) which they required.

In 1837 the Act was passed. It stated that a Board of Commissioners was to be established, with membership drawn from the millowners and landowners affected. It was the intention that the dams would provide an even flow of water, with the stipulation that the night time flow should be one half of the day time flow. They were to be allowed to raise share capital of £40,000, with a further £30,000 to be raised by a mortgage charge on the water rates to be levied. The Act provided for up to eight reservoirs, but in the event only three were built; one at Holme Styles and one at Bowshaw Whams, both near to Hade Edge village; the third was built on the Digley stream and was to be known as Bilberry Reservoir after the small berried fruit shrub which flourished (and still does) in profusion on the moors. With the benefit of hindsight it is clear that the sum allowed for the construction of the huge dam walls was completely inadequate.

Bilberry Reservoir was completed in 1840 about two kilometres upstream from Holmbridge, at a point about 150 metres from the confluence of two rivers flowing from the mountainside. It enclosed a wide area of some fifteen to twenty acres (depending on the water levels). The dam wall was built where the valley sides narrowed and was 20 metres above the river bed at its highest point and 100 metres across. It drained an area of some 14000 acres of moorland around Holme Moss and Saddleworth.

The core of the dam wall was an impermeable mix of materials, called 'puddle', which was five metres thick at the bottom tapering to two and a half metres thick at the top. A tunnel led from the base of the reservoir to allow a controlled quantity of water to flow through to the river. A stone lined waste pit, or bye wash, (in effect a chimney for the water) was built to one side of the dam wall, leading down to the tunnel. At the base of the chimney were two shuttles, parallel vertical trapdoors, to regulate the flow. The shuttles were raised and lowered together by means of perpendicular rods controlled from a platform at the top of the waste pit. If the water level became too high in spite of these controls, the excess water would overflow down the chimney of the waste pit.

A serious problem was encountered during the building of the dam wall. Whilst blasting was taking place to create a firm foundation for the 'puddle' a small spring was uncovered, about the thickness of a man's arm. At the inquest it became the basis of a vital disagreement; the workmen who found the spring reported it, they said, but the Engineer in charge of the project said that he was unaware of it. The workmen waited five or six weeks for the Engineer to respond to the problem, at a cost, it was estimated, of £200 to £300 before they went ahead and completed the dam wall.

Within a few years it became clear that repairs were required. The middle of the dam wall had settled down and sunk so low that it was below the level of the top of the waste pit. This overflow 'chimney' was thus rendered completely useless, and in consequence excess water would flow over the middle of the dam wall and erode the embankment.

A dispute arose between the original contractors and the Reservoir Commissioners and in 1848 new contractors were appointed to carry out the repairs. They opened up the embankment to assess the work required to resolve the problem caused by the spring. After investigation they informed the Commissioners that they would need to excavate more material so that they could divert the spring away from the embankment. However, the Commissioners were facing financial problems and instructed the engineers to refill the dam wall with 'puddle' to complete the work. It turned out to be a tragic misjudgement.

It seems that this was the first (and most serious) of a catalogue of errors, caused by bad management, poor communications and lack of money. The dam was leaky and news of this became common knowledge in the Valley. The number and intensity of the leaks increased. Over the years following the reconstruction £1500 was spent on further work to repair the fault but with little success. Maintenance of the shuttles lapsed so that they became blocked with stones and other mountain debris, thus rendering them ineffective for the regulation of water flow. In spite of the repairs, the centre of the dam wall had subsided again so that it was below the level of the waste pit. All in all, management seems to have been very lax and ineffective, and this became a significant fact in the subsequent inquest. The scene was set for the tragic flood which devastated the Holme Valley.

January, 1852 produced long periods of sustained rain, a not unusual occurrence in the Pennine areas. The rain continued into February, with the result that Bilberry Reservoir rapidly filled up, and surplus water was unable to flow away. No rainfall statistics were made for the area, but five miles away, over the mountain in Woodhead, the rainfall was impressive. Ten inches of rain (about 25 centimetres) fell in the first nine days of February; of more significance, in the 24 hour period between 11am on Wednesday 4th and 11am Thursday 5th, 2.4 inches (about 6 centimetres) were recorded. We can safely assume that the rain over the moors at the head of the Holme valley was likely to be of similar proportions.

On Sunday, 1st February it was becoming clear that the reservoir was filling up and the overflow systems were not coping with the excess. A workman had been engaged early in February to clean out the shuttles to allow a clear outflow of water. Tragically, the urgency of the work was not understood, nor were adequate instructions given. As a result the workman had suspended his work in order to clarify who would be paying him.

The heavy rainfall resulted in a rapid build up of water levels in the Reservoir. It was also noted that there strong winds, all the day and into the evening. At six o'clock on Wednesday evening, 4th February, the water had risen to within eight feet (2.5 metres) of the top of the embankment. By nine o'clock there was only two feet (0.6 metre) of clearance, and by midnight the water was gently lapping over the top of the reservoir wall. Significantly, it was also noted that water was seeping through to the riverbed from underneath the embankment; this was the fatal flaw which the builders had tried unsuccessfully to correct. Parts of the embankment were washed away and large fissures appeared in the wall.

By midnight it was too late to avoid a tragic disaster. The reservoir was full to the brim with, it is estimated, 86 million gallons of water (390 million litres), weighing in at about 390,000 tonnes. Water was still flowing down the mountain sides into the reservoir, although the rain had stopped falling a few hours previously, before nightfall. The clouds had blown away and the reservoir was bathed in an eerie, almost romantic, moonlight. Even up to midnight a few spectators had sensed the danger and had come to watch out and wait for the tragedy which now seemed to be inevitable.

The people in the valley had been aware of the potential danger for some time. However, each danger point had passed before and an attitude of resigned acceptance was common. Some of the inhabitants of Water Street had been warned earlier the same day that it would be wise not to go to bed that night. Their response was 'We have heard that tale before'.

Since the rain had been stopped for a few hours and bright moonlight was bathing the valley, it looked like another false alarm, even though a strong wind was blowing. Only a few people, as they climbed up to survey the Reservoir on that fateful evening, began to realize that this was no longer a false alarm. They were looking at a tragedy in the making and they were too late to warn the people now sleeping in Holmfirth and the other villages on the floor of the Holme Valley.

The pressure on the reservoir built up until, just before one o'clock on the morning of February 5th, there was a roar like thunder and the embankment wall was forced out, like a cork from a bottle, to flood the valley. The water under the embankment had turned into mud and, acting as a lubricant, undermined the whole structure. One witness described the scene as the rising of an immense sheet of mist accompanied by a rumbling sound like thunder. Within thirty minutes the whole reservoir emptied as 390,000 tonnes of water overwhelmed the valley.

CHAPTER 3

DESTRUCTION IN THE VALLEY
5ᵀᴴ FEBRUARY, 1852

When the embankment wall was so disastrously undermined on that fateful night, only those living close to the reservoir had any real warning of the disaster to come. These families had all managed, in the final few minutes, to scramble to safer places higher up the valley sides. Even so, they left with only the most meagre of possessions, usually the clothes or night attire they were wearing.

The full extent of the mounting danger was realised only in the last half hour and it was not possible to relay notice of the threat to the town of Holmfirth, now sleeping, three miles away. Three messengers set out to run to the beleaguered town, and one, John Whitely, just managed to reach Upperbridge at about the same time as the floodwaters. He had been able to raise the alarm to some of the communities en route and his warnings had been heeded. He collapsed as he reached the town, but even in this exhausted state he was able to provide some little warning; but it was too late to be effective.

Digley Mill   Upper Digley Mill   Bilberry Mill

The first mill in the destructive path of the waters as they surged out of the shattered dam wall was Bilberry Mill, a substantial three storey fulling mill; however it was set a little to one side up the slope and so only the gable end was carried away. The miller, or mill manager, (who was also in charge of the shuttles for the reservoir) was called Charles Battye and he lived in a cottage adjoining the mill. He had sent his family away for safety and had carefully removed his furniture for security nearby. He escaped from his cottage, just in time to see his furniture swept away. His near neighbour, Joseph Charlesworth, the mill engineer, lived in a cottage just above the water's flow and he escaped unharmed.

When the waters eventually subsided the valley was covered nearly three metres deep in rubble, mainly from the embankment wall. The remains of the mill were covered as high as the second floor of the building. Bilberry bridge was swept away completely and the river bed filled with rubble.

Some 300 metres further down the valley stood Upper Digley Mill. At the time of the flood it was in the hands of the Bailiffs of the Leeds Bankruptcy Court. It too was slightly offset so that only the end of the building and the gable end of the adjoining house were destroyed. A small farm adjacent to the mill was completely overwhelmed. The remains of the machinery and stock of rolls of cloth from the mill were strewn down the valley. There was no loss of life, but the mill manager, who had been confined to his bed for the preceding seven weeks, had to stay in one end of his ruined cottage overnight (with his wife and three children) until he could be taken away by cart.

The Ruins of Digley Mill, with the chimney still intact. This chimney lasted for nearly another 100 years, even surviving the 1944 flood (Sam Massey/Fountain of Leeds)

A further 300 metres downstream was the substantial four storey premises of Digley Mill, which included a water wheel and steam engine, and was built directly on the riverside. It took the full impact of the deluge and the buildings were completely destroyed. The solid stone-built mill housed 34 power looms along with other machinery and stocks of cloth in process; in addition there were two dwellinghouses and seven cottages, a farm (including some unfortunate farm animals) and other outbuildings. On the other side of the river were extensive dyeworks. The force of the water was such that everything was swept away and some machinery, weighing 10 to 12 tons was found nearly a mile away in Hinchliffe Mill. Surprisingly, the tall chimney attached to the mill survived; the story goes that it was shifted bodily ten metres from its original position!

It was fortunate that all the inhabitants of the properties had managed to move higher up the valley sides. One man and his wife and children escaped with only the clothes on their backs, together with half a loaf of bread and an old crust of cheese. Another young man, confined to his bed by rheumatism, was wrapped in a blanket and carried by four men up to a neighbour's house just a minute before his house was swept away.

Mrs Hirst, the widow of the late owner of Digley Mill had tried to seek comfort that evening by reading in her Bible about the troubles of Job. When she was told of the potential flood she responded by saying that she might as well go with her house, but after some thought she took the precaution of moving small household items into the rooms upstairs, but leaving heavy furniture, including a piano, in the 'lower room'.

Mrs Hirst was an indomitable lady. She sought safety herself down in the cellar, which is not the ideal position with an impending flood looming. Only the swift and forceful action of her neighbours persuaded her to leave the cellar. She snatched up her youngest child, who was in bed, wrapped him in a table cloth and they all hurried out over a wooden bridge to safety.

They escaped with seconds to spare, but Mrs Hirst recalled later the sight of a wall of water, 'mountains high', bearing down on them - and seeing her white window blinds carried away on the water. She had about £50 in gold and silver coins in the house and all were lost.

Not everything was permanently lost; some of her treasured possessions were found and preserved. She had a china cabinet full of blue ware, which was later recovered intact from the mud. But more important, her precious Bible was found, complete with the spectacles which she had been wearing. She had used the spectacles as a book mark, lodged in the pages of the Book of Judges. The Bible was given to her daughter, who carefully cleaned it to remove as much as possible of the mud from that dreadful night. The spectacles had been in place so long that they had corroded and left their imprint on the pages of her Bible. Years later her granddaughter presented the Bible to Holmbridge Church as a reminder of the night of the flood, with pages still showing where the spectacles had rested and rusted.

Just below Digley Mill stood Bank End Mill, another substantial stone-built four storey property, abutting the river. The end of the building was carried away by the water and the weaving looms and spinning mules on the upper floors slid down towards the gap and were left projecting from the ruin. A small mill dam wall gave away and added further floodwater. There was no loss of life and the owner had had the foresight to remove most of his stocks of woollen cloth.

After Bank End Mill stands the village of Holmbridge, where the valley widens out a little; just sufficient width nowadays for a cricket field. This took some of the force from the water, although not enough to prevent the road near the bridge from being washed away, leaving the bridge foundations exposed. The arch of the bridge was left intact, but a plank was needed for the next few months for local inhabitants and visitors to walk across. St David's Church, a recent structure situated in the middle of the graveyard, withstood the worst damage, although it was flooded inside to a depth of about 1.5 metres. The stone floor was torn up and pews were floated about, along with bibles and hymn books and cushions, and with a layer of mud deposited on the floor.

The church goat, which used to feed in the churchyard, had been washed into the centre aisle. More distressing was the coffin and body of a full grown man, carried from the graveyard and also deposited in the church. All the houses near to the church were covered in mud and the debris of broken machinery, looms, boilers, cloth, yarn, furniture, stones and hay, together with the corpses of animals from the farms; there was also an overpowering stench which lingered foully for weeks.

CHAPTER 4

DEATH IN THE VALLEY

For the first five minutes after the dam wall collapsed no lives were lost, although the destruction had been enormous. The impending disaster had been signalled down the valley as far as Holmbridge (which at the time they spelt Holmebridge). Beyond this point, however, the valley narrowed with precipitous cliffs at one side or the other. This hemmed in the water and caused it to rise and increase in speed and power, reinforced by the weight of debris carried along. It sped into the village of Hinchliffe Mill, where houses were built alongside the north side of the river on Ford Gate (then called Fold Gate) and Water Street. The mill was built on the opposite side, to take advantage of the river to power the watermill.

All that remained of the bridge at Holmebridge, (now spelt Holmbridge), from a position near St. Davids Church

The road crosses the river at this point, on a bridge built in 1838 (or thereabouts; the last figure in indistinct). The arch of stone across the river survived, with the date still discernable on the keystone. However the water flooded the houses alongside the bridge in Fordgate up to the level of the first floor, and residents were trapped inside. But much worse was to follow. As the river approaches the mill it veers to the right, just a little, as it passes the mill dam. The full impact of the surging water from the reservoir went straight on at this point, and demolished six three storey houses backing on to the river's edge but with frontages on Water Street.

It was a major tragedy. 44 people from six families lived in the stone built cottages; 36 were drowned, men, women and children. The flood was so swift and powerful that only eight managed to escape. A further five perished on Ford Gate, making 41 drowned; half of the total lost on that terrible night. One eye witness reported that he saw the water come rolling down the valley; in a minute he saw the cottages tremble, as it were, on the top of the water, and the next moment they were clean gone. Another eye witness uses very similar wording. He saw the six houses wobble a bit like on the top of the water, and then they all went down.

We shall never know the exact details of what went on in those few seconds of destruction, but we do know of some miraculous escapes. Three of the Charlesworth children ran out of the back of their house to the door of a neighbour living opposite, Robert Ellis. He let them in and shut the door, which was immediately forced open by the power of the water. It rose some feet up in the ground floor, but he and the children (three Charlesworths and some of his own) managed to run upstairs and escape at the top of the house. Two other Charlesworth children returned to rescue two pet hens, and were drowned; a tragic loss which shows how swiftly the calamity overcame them.

Robert Ellis's own baby was overlooked in the rush. However a neighbour, Charles Johnson, found him in a waterlogged cradle, under a table. He was taken to the 'New Inn' (later 'The Bareknuckle Boys' and now 'The Shepherd's Rest') and they were able to revive him. The effect on Mrs Ellis was extreme, even though in the end all her family survived; she became deranged for a few months until her mind could begin the grasp the scope of the tragedy.

James Mettrick (24 years of age) managed to put on his trousers and helped the children in his household to move upstairs from their bedroom downstairs. This was accomplished just before the water burst into the downstairs room. They had moved to the safety, so they thought, of the garret in the roof of the house, but after half a minute the whole of the house collapsed and was swept away, together with all the inhabitants. They were all washed downstream and the children were drowned.

Somehow James was lucky; he managed to keep his head above water until he found himself half a mile (800 metres) downstream in the mill dam of Harpin's (now Bottoms) Mill. He caught hold of a large piece of wood and inhaled a good breath of fresh air. He lost his hold on the wood, but clung on to another plank and paddled himself towards the edge of the mill dam, completely exhausted. His father, also James Mettrick, was drowned but his body was not found until five months later.

Joseph Brook was rescued, but his wife and daughter died. His daughter had woken up and ran downstairs to tell her father that she was frightened by the wind. Joseph realised that it was not the wind that she heard; it was the sound of rushing water. He told her to rush upstairs and he fled there himself; when he turned round neither his wife nor daughter were there. They were later found, drowned, huddled together on the bed where his daughter had fled for safety.

George Crosland sent his family upstairs, but he was caught downstairs. Luckily the water did not reach as far as the roof and he managed to hold on to a 'sampler' hung up in a frame; this held firm until he was rescued.

The devastation was so swift and unexpected that the events of those few seconds were a complete confusion. Most of the children were fast asleep and there was little time to rouse them to escape. The noise of the water in full spate sounded like the wind and those who were able to see the flood as it advanced noted the debris of destroyed properties and machinery in the wall of water as it overwhelmed them. Most of them did not live to tell the tale.

Mr Jos F Massers drawing of the houses and mills alongside the river from Victoria (left) upstream to Hinchliffe Mill, As they were before the flood.

Dysons Mill occupied by Mr Sandford
Victoria Mill
Bottoms Mill
Lower Hinchill Mill and Water Street
Bridge
School Room

The Hinchliffe Mill building was flooded up to second floor level, but survived. However much stock and machinery was swept away to add to the debris carried down the valley.

At Bottoms Mill, where James Mettrick found himself, no lives were lost, but the inhabitants of a row of three cottages only escaped by breaking through the thin stone partition wall and climbing down a ladder at the end of the cottage farthest away from the river. Five fullers on duty overnight were marooned half submerged in the rafters of the mill until the flood had subsided.

A further 300 metres downstream were more factories, including an iron foundry. Adjacent to Victoria Mill (opposite to where the Victoria pub is at present) were three adjoining cottages with warehouse premises over the top. They were surrounded by water and one family, the Pogsons, climbed up by ladder into the attic. They broke through the thin wall into the warehouse and then through the floor of the building to bring up the second family, the Sandersons. They hoped to escape via an outside flight of steps but to their horror these had been washed away. As they waited their fear grew as both cottages gave way under the pressure of the water.

The family in the third cottage, the Howards, could not find their way upstairs into the warehouse, so all three families (about 20 people) were marooned on a dwindling floor space, some in the cottage and some in the warehouse overhead. When the waters had subsided a little they managed to find a ladder and escaped down the end wall. They were able to climb out just in time before the roof fell in and the rest of the building collapsed.

Close to Victoria Mill stood Dyson's Mill, with a dwelling house in the mill yard occupied by the owner, Jonathan Sandford. He was a widower and lived with his two daughters (aged five and ten) and a housekeeper. Jonathan Sandford had prospered; in the few days preceding the flood he had arranged with a Huddersfield Stockbroker to buy a large amount of stock in the London and North Western Railway. He had just been negotiating the purchase of a considerable estate near Penistone, and his life was said to be insured for £1000. At the time of the flood it was thought that he had the sum of between £3000 and £4000 in his house. Although he had received warning of the state of the reservoir, he decided that he and his family would be safe that night at home.

In the event he lost everything: his family, his factory and his fortune. A reward was offered by the family for the recovery of his remains, so that the Life Assurance could be claimed, but it was over two weeks before his body was found.

Mr Sandford and his family attended the Wesleyan Chapel in Holmfirth. His two wives had been buried there, and his family tomb was there to receive the new occupants. The Minister, Rev W Firth, spoke affectionately of Mr Sandford and of the awful catastrophe by which so many homes had been made desolate.

Nearer to the town centre of Holmfirth the floodwaters washed away the two mills known as Upper Mill (near Prickleden) and Lower Mill the latter was built across the river. Both were substantial properties, and included a boiler with an estimated weight of six tons which was carried four miles downstream as far as Berry Brow. Upper Mill was occupied by Mr John Farrar. He had just drawn £700 from the bank, which had been left in his counting-house overnight. It was all lost and never recovered.

After Lower Mill the valley narrows, forcing the waters higher and with greater intensity as they descended on to the houses at Scarfold. This is a few metres upstream from Upperbridge where the old road crosses the river into Hollowgate. From this point the river runs alongside the road into the centre of Holmfirth. The underdwellings at Scarfold face on to the river, but the upper dwellings face on to the main road, the Turnpike road, now called Woodhead Road. Scarfold received the full fury of the engorged river.

Mr Lomax, a surgeon, heard the exhausted calls of alarm from John Whitely, who had run down the valley as already mentioned. He just managed to save his wife and family by via a back window into higher ground. John Charlesworth also managed to escape and helped out his recently confined wife and his two children to the Turnpike Road. He returned to retrieve some of his furniture, only to see his house and contents carried away by the flood. Just a few seconds later and he would also have been engulfed.

His next door neighbour, Richard Woodcock, was not so fortunate. He went to the Turnpike Road to find out the cause of the alarm, then hastily returned to the house. His wife handed him two children, whom he carried under his arm and left on the road. He returned to the house and found that his wife had climbed the ladder to the garret room to save her other five children three in one bed and two in the other. Two of the three-to-a-bed had got out a girl of five and a lad of seventeen. The boy, Alfred, had gone back upstairs to put on his trousers (a remarkable display of modesty in the circumstances), whilst the girl was rescued; she was held aloft by her mother, who was standing up to her neck in water.

The ladder to the garret was washed away, leaving four children in the attic. One boy, with trousers on, and his twelve year old sister were carried away when part of the floor collapsed. The other two children (aged eight and fifteen), in the separate bed, were safe, as the floor at one end was still intact. In all, out of a family of nine, seven survived (father, mother and five children) whilst two were drowned. The body of a twelve year old girl, thought to be Sarah Woodcock, was only found around 1990.

Joseph Hellawell, with his wife and five young children, were asleep when the flood waters overwhelmed their house, an underdwelling on Scarfold. Joseph was swept upstairs into his weaving room, where he managed to hang on and cry for help. He was pulled to safety through the ceiling into the floor of the house above. Later his neighbour found the bodies of his wife and children, who had been trapped in their bedroom.

CHAPTER 5

DEVASTATION IN THE TOWN CENTRE

It was only a quarter of an hour after the Reservoir collapsed before the flood waters hit Holmfirth, at Scarfold and Upperbridge. By the time they reached the town centre the waters had been turned into a battering ram by the addition of heavy machinery, stones, fabric, dead farm animals and tons of earth which had been scooped away as the flood progressed. In spite of heroic efforts very little warning of the impending disaster reached the town centre. It was 1.15 in the morning and most of the inhabitants were asleep.

In Upperbridge and Hollowgate the stories of disasters and miraculous escapes continued. Aner Bailey saw his wife and two children swept away before his eyes; he managed to cling on to a beam and was deposited on to the Turnpike Road. In Hollowgate the floodwaters were hemmed in by buildings and in consequence increased in height. In the Toll Bar House Samuel Greenwood was seen to come to the door, with a lighted candle, to look for the cause of all the noise. He hastily closed the door, but in vain. The building was washed away, along with Samuel, his wife and niece, Eliza Matthews, a girl of twelve.

Ruins of Upperbridge and half of the Pub (now rebuilt as The Elephant and Castle)
(Illustrated London News)

Henry Parson was a baby living with his parents at Upperbridge. He was rescued, along with his family, after they carried him up into the attic of their house overlooking

24

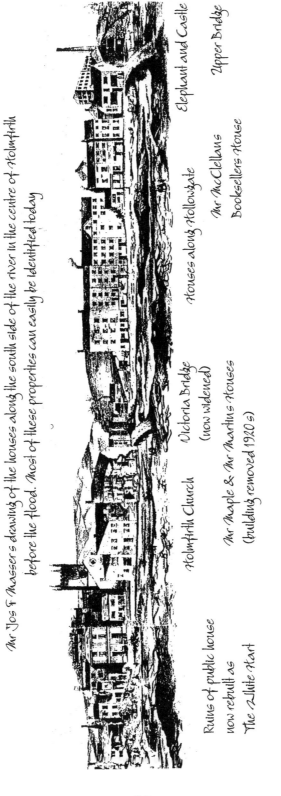

Mr Jos F Moser's drawing of the houses along the south side of the river in the centre of Holmfirth before the flood. Most of these properties can easily be identified today

Ruins of public house now rebuilt as The White Hart

Holmfirth Church

Mr Maple & Mr Martins Houses (building removed 1920 s)

Victoria Bridge (now widened)

Houses along Hollowgate

Mr McClellans Booksellers House

Elephant and Castle

Upper Bridge

the river. Years later he recounted this story to his children and grandchildren, and it is still remembered today by his granddaughter, Mrs Audrey Helm, now herself an old lady in her eighties and living in Almondbury.

Mrs Elizabeth Kippax, the landlady of the Elephant and Castle pub, just across the river from the Tollhouse at Upperbridge, was lucky. She, along with her servants Mary and Grace Spivey had tried to escape through the doors. The floodwaters held them firmly in place, but they all managed to scramble up to the garret until the level of the waters had fallen.

John Ashall, a leather currier (one who dresses and colours tanned leather), lived near the toll house with his wife Margaret and young son Alfred. They were awakened to the dangers and tried to dress and escape; a neighbour heard their cries for help, but the house collapsed and they were all drowned before anyone could reach them.

John Kaye, a grocer and corndealer, lived next door to the Ashalls with his daughter, (Amelia Fearnes), son in law and granddaughter, a six month old baby called Lydia Ann. Amelia was carrying Lydia Ann and both were drowned when the house collapsed. Her husband Matthew was swept away and found later in a totally exhausted state in Holmfirth churchyard. He was rescued by Joseph Barraclough, who took him to his own house in South Lane to recover. John Kaye himself was carried down into Victoria Square where the landlord of the Rose and Crown Inn pulled him to safety by means of a flagpole thrust out of his window.

Joseph Barraclough was a hero that night. He was on hand later to help William Martin (a jeweller and watchmaker) and his family to escape from their shop on Victoria Street, near to the bridge. William threw out his children from the first floor room down to Joseph, one by one. Joseph then somehow managed to procure a ladder to help down Mr and Mrs Martin. Then he helped William's neighbours to escape to safety. He was indeed a busy man that night.

There were some remarkable escapes from the premises on Hollowgate. Mr Thomas Ellis, a plumber, managed to escape by breaking open the ceiling of his workshop and climbing into the room of the premises above. Richard Tolson, in the same building with his wife, four children and a lodger, were trapped in a bedroom. They escaped by climbing up a small bedroom chimney into the premises above.

On Rotcher (a small road leading up from Hollowgate) James Lee (a tailor) and his grandson Job were working, making clothes for a funeral. James was drowned, but Job was saved by his sister and her husband, who heard his cries for help and broke open a door panel with their feet to drag him to safety through a five inch aperture.

In Victoria Square the buildings and the bridge were badly damaged. Those who stayed in their houses were fearful as they felt the substantial stone premises rock and sway as the floodwaters rushed through their lower rooms. Nearby in Cuttell Bottom a man was sleeping, with his little boy. Whilst he was trying to save the boy they became separated as the water forced shut a door with the boy still inside and he was given up for dead. Providentially the waters carried him up to the roof and he managed to cling

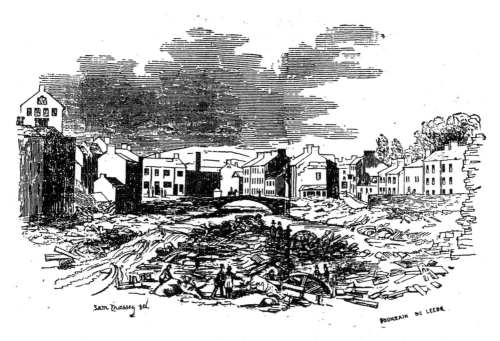

Piles of broken machinery and dead farm animals scattered across the centre of
Holmfirth in Hollowgate. Looking upstream towards Uppergate and Scarfold.
(Sam Massey/Fountain of Leeds)

REMAINS OF BRIDGE, AND SITE OF TOLL-HOUSE.

All that remained of the Main Town Bridge (now Victoria Square) looking downstream
towards the church. The houses on the centre right, built on to the river bank, were
demolished in the 1920s. (Illustrated London News)

to the joists for an hour with the water nearly up to the ceiling.

Edward Williamson had just opened a shop at the bottom of Victoria Street, near to the river. He was awoken by the flood, which was up to the level of his bedroom. He hurriedly dressed and escaped by climbing on to a narrow ledge outside his shop and edging along for a few yards. He eventually jumped and luckily a bale of wool broke his fall. Mrs Woodcock, a neighbour of Edward, took the same escape route and shuffled along past eight shops to safety.

She then found that her family had not followed, as she had thought, so she edged back again to rescue them. On the way she lost her balance and fell into the bedroom window of one of the shops. Later she found that her house had survived, along with her husband and children.

Holmfirth Parish Church stands back a little way from the road and did not suffer extensive damage. However one indication of the power of the flood is shown by the

Great Storm, Holmfirth, looking towards Victoria Square. (Illustrated London News)

fact that one of the massive pillars of the gateway was lifted bodily upwards, twisted round yet remained in the perpendicular.

Holmfirth Mill, a four storey structure built on the site now occupied by the Post Office, sustained serious damage and two cottages nearby were completely destroyed. Although only two families were involved, this small area suffered twelve deaths. One cottage was occupied by Sidney Hartley his wife and eight children and an apprentice called John Dearnley - and the other by Richard Shackleton, his wife and three children. Only four of this small group survived.

Mrs Hartley had heeded the warnings about the Bilberry Dam, and sat up so that she could save her children, if it was necessary. But at one o'clock the danger seemed to have receded and she went to bed - just a quarter of an hour too early. She tried to save her infant child, a boy of just 10 weeks, by holding him outside the window of her house, but she and the house were swept away. Only three of her children survived, together with the apprentice who helped to save them. David, the eldest son, had climbed on to the roof of the house by removing some of the stone slates; he was able to pull through his sister Ann and brother James, as well as the apprentice. David was unable to rescue any more but he saw his mother wish him goodbye just before she was carried away. They all clung to rafters of the roof for twenty minutes before they were able, one by one, to clamber into the safety of the Mill yard; cold and miserable, but alive.

Two local worthies lived in the centre of town. Eldon House, on the left bank of the river opposite Towngate (and on the site of the present Old Bridge Inn) was the home of Joseph Charlesworth, Esq., JP. The house was at one stage entirely surrounded by water; considerable damage was done, but there was no loss of life. Mr Joshua Moorhouse, Esq., JP had his residence in Victoria yard; his extensive warehouses and mills were destroyed, but he escaped unharmed.

Opposite the White Hart Inn lived Mr Shackleton, a retired publican and the father of Richard Shackleton, who was drowned with his family, as noted above. He lived with his daughter and granddaughter. William Dyson, the landlord of the White Hart and a friend of the family, brought them out of their house and into the pub just in time to save them as their house was submerged by the floodwaters. William Dyson was another hero, as he took in four occupants from cottages damaged at Mill Hill.

Norridge Bottom is the quaint name given to the underdwellings located behind the Old Bridge Hotel. It was and is quite low lying, and was quickly inundated up to the level of the first floor. However, its location behind other buildings meant that the full fury of the waters had been curbed a little. It was occupied by poor Irish hawkers with few possessions. They all managed to hang on to their properties and their lives. Two women and four children clung on to a bed as it was hurled around in their bedroom. Two men were hauled by rope to the houses above. Eight members of another family climbed up the chimney to safety in the floor above.

Eli Sanderson, the owner of the houses on Norridge Bottom, heard the waters approaching and carried two of his children to safety. When he returned, seconds later, he found the first floor under water. Providentially all the family were saved as Mrs Sanderson had managed to take all the other children up into the attic.

On the opposite side of the river to the Holmfirth Mill stood the old Wesleyan Chapel, built in 1810 and surrounded by a graveyard. The chapel was flooded to pew height, but the ministers and their families, living just a little higher up the slope, were just clear of danger. Several coffins were washed up from the graveyard. Of particular poignancy was the fate of Mr John Harpin; his vault was torn open and his coffin, his resting place for ten years, floated downstream with his remains. Ironically Mr Harpin was the owner of Harpin's Mill, near Hinchliffe Mill, and was one of the chief promoters for the building of the Bilberry Reservoir

Beyond Holmfirth the floodwaters lost some of their ferocity, although they were still capable of serious damage. Broadbent's fulling mill was destroyed, as was the County bridge leading to the railway station, built only a few years before. At Thongsbridge a mill and dyehouse were carried away. The engineer on site sprang to the window to escape the water; he just managed to catch hold of his son by the leg as he floated out of the door beside him.

Mytholmbridge Mill suffered serious damage, as did Smithy Place Mill at Brockholes. The water rose to a fearful height, but sufficient warning had been given for everyone to escape (although only in their night attire), except for a small eight year old girl. The rampaging water continued with destructive force to Honley and Armitage Bridge, but luckily without any further loss of life, although bodies from up the valley were deposited near the Golden Fleece Inn at Armitage Bridge.

When the sun rose in the following morning the full extent of the damage and destruction could be seen. It was a fearful sight. As the waters passed and subsided they left behind heaps of mud, stones, turnips, machinery, boilers, rollers, bodies of horses, cattle and sheep, fabric, and a few human remains, all piled haphazardly over the floor of the valley. The valley folk now had to begin to rebuild their lives after one of the most severe civil disasters of the reign of Queen Victoria.

CHAPTER 6

THE AFTERMATH - AND THE INQUEST

As dawn broke on that fateful Thursday morning, the life of the Holme Valley had been completely transformed. The people had to recover and rebuild their lives from a disaster of a ferocity which few could have imagined. The first gruesome task in the rebuilding was to find and bury their dead. Their second task was to grieve and mourn for the families so cruelly torn apart.

Bodies had been scattered along the Holme Valley and beyond, some being eventually found as far away as Wakefield. It took some days, even weeks before the corpses were recovered, although one was only located about 140 years later. The bodies which could immediately be found were taken to public houses down the valley, to await burial. The results of the widespread devastation can be deduced from the location of the bodies, miles from their habitations.

New Inn (now The Shepherds Rest)	Hinchliffe Mill	9
George Inn	Holmfirth	9
Elephant and Castle	Holmfirth	5
White Hart	Holmfirth	6
Shoulder of Mutton	Holmfirth	3
Rose and Crown	Holmfirth	1
King's Head		1
Waggon and Horses		2
Crown Hotel		7
Rose and Crown	Thongsbridge	3
Royal Oak	Thongsbridge	5
Rock Inn	Smithy Place	2
Travellers' Inn	Honley	4
Jacob's Well	Honley	4
Golden Fleece	Armitage Bridge	2
Oddfellows Arms	Big Valley	1

This catalogue of tragedy shows that only 64 bodies were recovered in the immediate vicinity. Families had been torn asunder, even in death. For instance, the Mettrick family, seven of them from Water Street, Hinchliffe Mill, were scattered; one was in the Wagon and Horses, one in the Rock Inn, one in the Travellers' Inn. The four other members of the family were not even mentioned in the first listing.

Some of the bodies were unidentified at this stage; it seems likely that no family member was available to travel down the valley for such a grim but necessary task. The bodies at the Golden Fleece at Armitage Bridge, for instance, a boy and a girl, were both unidentified. The body of the little girl was the subject of anguished discussion. At first it was claimed as Jane Mettrick, aged four; then thought to be either Elizabeth Hartley (aged four), or Ellen Ann Hartley (aged two), Eventually it was claimed and

31

buried as Ann Bailey, daughter of Aner Bailey. We can well understand the distress caused by the uncertainly in these situations.

About 60 of the deceased were buried on Sunday, 8th February in the villages in the Valley. It was a sombre day for all concerned. At Holmbridge, where the Churchyard had been flooded and graves forced open by the waters, the coffins had to remain in the Church until the ground had been restored to a fit condition.

The sorrow, almost palpable in the funeral services in the valley, was prolonged for some families, where bodies were still to be found. James Mettrick, senior, from Water Street, Hinchliffe Mill, was found five months later on the river bank at Castleford, thirty miles away. It was two or three days before Mr Sandford's two children and housekeeper were found, but two weeks before Jonathan Sandford himself was discovered. It was buried so deeply in the mud at Thongsbridge that it looked, it was said, like a big joint of bacon. It took half an hour of struggle for three men to release the body, which had a linen nightshirt wound tightly round the head.

We can only imagine the torment of those drowned in the flood. Perhaps it was lucky that they had been swept away during the night. Many of the children would have been drowned as they slept, and would have been almost unaware of the event. The devastation was so sudden that many of the adults would have had little time to take in the enormity of the disaster they were facing. Witnesses noted that most of the children looked serene and calm, as their bodies were collected, whereas the adults seemed to be full of surprise and consternation. It was some small consolation that the suddenness of the inundation had kept the terror of the victims to a minimum.

In all, 81 people, men, women, children and tiny babies, were drowned. A full list, with ages, reveals the full extent of the tragedy which had fallen on the Holme Valley.

The saddest part of the deaths was that whole families were wiped out. 41 people from Hinchliffe Mill were drowned, mainly from the aptly named Water Street, where six cottages were completely destroyed. These family names are still to be found in the valley.

Of the families which were drowned, there were:

4 Marsdens	(father, mother, two teenage sons)	
4 Dodds	(father, mother, two girls, aged seven and one)	
8 Croslands	(father, two teenage sons, three teenage daughters, two younger boys)	
7 Charlesworths	(father, mother, two teenage boys, three younger children) but three children survived.	
7 Mettricks	(father, mother, brother, three sons one daughter) but seven children survived.	
5 Earnshaws	(grandfather, father, daughter, grandson, granddaughter)	

together with six others (with names of Heeley, Brook, Booth and Beaumont). Some of the families were intermarried, so devastating at one blow more than one family.

Memorial to the dead. These were often printed in silver or gold on black paper, as a suitable sign of mourning

Further down the valley, at Victoria and Holmfirth, a further 40 were drowned:

3 Sandfords   (father, two young girls)
6 Hellawells (mother, two young boys, two young girls, baby girl 9 mths)
2 Woodcocks   (sister and brother)
3 Baileys   (mother, two young girls)
7 Hartleys   (father, mother, two teenage children, two young girls,
              one baby boy, 10 weeks)
              but four children survived.
5 Shackletons (father, mother, two young girls, one baby boy)
3 Greenwoods (father, mother, child)
              together with 11 others, all with local names (Wood, Ashall,
              Fearns, Thorpe, Lee, Heeley).

We can see how the flood took away the lives across all ages, but chiefly amongst the children:

	Males	Females	Total
Babies one year and under	3	4	7
Young Children up to 9	10	13	23
Children 10 to 19	7	8	15
Adults 20 to 29	2	5	7
30 to 39	6	7	13
40 to 49	5	3	8
over 50	4	1	5
	- - -	- - -	- - -
	37	41	78
No names or ages given			3
			- - -
			81
			===

Most bodies from the flood were eventually recovered, and given a decent Christian burial. One body was unaccounted for - Sarah Woodcock, a 12 year old girl from 9 Scarfold. This body was only found around 1990, whilst a goit to the mill pond at Sands was being cleared and drained. The age of the skeleton, and the fact that it was a young girl of approximately 12, both pointed to the strong possibility that this was Sarah's missing body.

The effect of such a heavy loss of life in such a small and close community would be devastating, and still casts a shadow over the years. The loss of time and talent which occurred will be having its effect down the Valley, even 150 years later.

The houses on Water Street, destroyed by the floodwaters, were never rebuilt; the gap in the houses remains. It is at a place where there is a slight bend in the river, just before it flows past the Mill. Because of the bend in the river the houses caught the full force of the water as it accelerated straight down the valley, and never stood a chance. Other houses, set just a few yards away, escaped the worst damage.

The list of damaged property was extensive. 83 building (Mills, dyehouses, cottages, bridges, warehouses, barns) were completely destroyed and a further 244 were seriously damaged. 200 acres of land were inundated and it was estimated that 10,000 persons were dependent on the destroyed properties. Over 7000 people (including more than 2100 children) were thrown out of work, with a loss of average weekly wages of £3,748 - about 53 new pence per person per week. The losses of property were originally estimated at £250,000 (equivalent to about £50,000,000 at today's values) but this was subsequently found to be an overestimate.

News of the Flood travelled far and wide and crowds in their thousands came to inspect the damage over the next few weeks. The Illustrated London News was able to carry a report within a month, complete with lithographs of the tragic scenes. The report must have been compiled in some haste, as some important names were misspelt; Digley was spelt 'Dighley' and Mettrick came out as 'Metternick'. The illustrations were not photographs, but rather tracings from photographs, so that much of the detail can be said to be authentic.

Another artist, Mr Jos F Masser, a lithographer of 25 Boar Lane, Leeds provided a 'Panoramic View of the Holmfirth and Digley Valley' showing all the properties along the riverbank, from Holmfirth all the way back to the Bilberry Reservoir itself; many of the buildings thus illustrated are still recognisable today. Around the lithograph were some miniature illustrations of the damage in more detail.

The local paper, 'The Huddersfield & Holmfirth Examiner' provided a map as part of fund raising efforts for the benefit of those who had suffered. The Huddersfield Chronicle issued a wall chart 'Scenes from the Holmfirth Catastrophe (which occurred on the morning of Feb. 5, 1852)' This was 'Presented Gratis to the Subscribers of the Huddersfield Chronicle'.

Most of these large lithographs were intended to be framed and hung on to parlour walls in memory of the tragic events. A few memorial tributes in the form of elaborately designed engravings, containing the names of all the dead, with their ages, were also issued. Some of these were printed in silver or gold on black paper to provide a suitable remembrance for the deceased, although the more conventional black on white were also printed.

There was widespread public sympathy throughout the country and £69,422 8s 4p (equivalent to about £14 million today) was raised to relieve the suffering. Over £31,000 was distributed amongst those who had incurred such grievous losses, although it was said that some sufferers made no claims upon the fund. The mortgagees of the Reservoir made a claim on these funds and after some dispute the sum of £7,000 was given for the repair of Bilberry Reservoir. The dispute arose following the Inquest jury's opinion of culpable negligence. It did not seem fair that the Mortgagees should profit from the negligence of the Commissioners. In the event the Reservoir was rebuilt, but on a smaller and safer scale.

Funds were also sufficient to build five Almshouses, which are still to be seen on Station Road on the New Mill road out of Holmfirth. After all costs and awards a balance of £31,011 11s 1p was returned to subscribers in January, 1854.   It is an amazing indication of the generosity of the public, and of the honesty of the Holme Valley inhabitants, that so much was raised, and so much subsequently returned.

The Central Committee which supervised the allocation of funds was unconstrained in praise of the generosity of the public in its final report:

'In presenting their final report and bringing their labours to a close, your committee desires to express the deep sense they entertain of the munificent liberality manifested by all classes of the British public in order to alleviate the sufferings occasioned by this sad accident…..
The parties who had subscribed thus liberally looked to your committee to see that their bounty was conferred on proper objects, and several of the towns placed only a portion of their subscriptions in the hands of your committee, reserving to themselves the appropriation of the remainder. These circumstances entailed …….. a large amount of responsibility, ……., and though the labour has not been small, the pleasure of becoming the medium of administering comfort to the sufferers ………. and preventing the ruin of great numbers of tradesmen, has amply compensated your committee………….. .'

The Inquest

An inquest had, of legal necessity, to be held on such an overwhelming tragedy. It was opened before the Coroner and a Jury of 16 on 6th February, only a day after the event itself.   It was adjourned to give the Jury the chance to see the recovered bodies and for the Government to appoint an Inspector to examine the damage to the reservoir. The Jury and Coroner reassembled at the White Hart Inn on 18th February, to hear the report of the Government Inspector, Captain Moody of the Royal Engineers, and to conclude the inquest.

It became clear from the Inspector's report that the management of the project to build and maintain the dam had been poor from the beginning. The root of the problem seemed to be financial, as construction costs were woefully underestimated, exacerbated by lack of experience. Few people had built reservoirs on this scale before. Maybe they thought that building a huge dam wall required more brawn than brain and as a consequence problems arising were not fully understood.

Whatever the reason, the Commissioners, who were responsible for the total management of the project, frequently overruled the instructions of the Engineer and seemed to be at odds with the foremen on site. One resigned after five months because he had not been paid. Financial restraints meant that the workers were inadequately paid and the Commissioners had at one stage to apply to Parliament for additional funds to complete the work.

The workers were left to their own devices for too long. It has already been noted that a spring was discovered when building the foundations, but the Engineer responsible denied that he knew anything about it. The Clerk of Works on site claimed to have sent in a fortnightly report on the progress of work; the Engineer could not remember receiving reports at such intervals. He even queried whether he was the responsible Engineer.   His site visits were infrequent and perfunctory.

Even when the work was completed the disputes did not end; they seemed to be a continuous feature of day to day management. The original contractors were replaced and claimed that they were still owed £3000 for building costs. Money was still due to the Bank and the Solicitors.   It has already been noted that extensive repairs were required in 1848 and had to be cut short because of lack of funds.   The Millowners refused to pay their water charges because they were not satisfied with the adequacy of the supply.

Company Law in England was at a primitive state. Legislation in relation to Joint Stock Companies was not passed until the 1850's and prior to that any venture requiring sizable amounts of finance had to be set up by Act of Parliament. This was a cumbersome and expensive procedure, since technically the Commissioners were responsible to Parliament for the construction and management of the building work.

The Jury gave their verdict on 27th February, after hearing the evidence and the report of the Government Inspector. They made their feelings very clear.

```
'We find that the deceased persons came to their deaths
by drowning, caused by the bursting of the Bilberry
reservoir. We also find that the Bilberry reservoir was
defective in its original construction, and that the
commissioners, the engineer, and the overlooker were
greatly culpable in not seeing to the proper regulation
of the works;  and we also find that the commissioners,
in permitting the Bilberry reservoir to remain for
several years in a dangerous state, with a full knowledge
thereof, and not lowering the waste pit, have been guilty
of great and culpable negligence;  and we regret that,
the reservoir being under the management of a
corporation, prevents us bringing in a verdict of
manslaughter, as we are convinced that the gross and
culpable negligence of the commissioners would have
subjected them to such a verdict had they been in the
position of an individual or firm. We also hope that the
Legislature will take into its most serious
consideration the propriety of making provision for the
protection of the lives and properties of her Majesty's
subjects exposed to danger from reservoirs placed by
corporations similar to those under the charge of the
Holme Reservoir Commissioners.'
```

In spite of the very clear statement above, no legislative action was taken. In 1864 an even more tragic event took place, when the Dale Dyke Reservoir near Sheffield burst its banks and 250 persons were drowned in the Loxley Valley. The cause of the bursting of the Reservoir was not clear, but it seems that water pipes under the embankment were leaking, and the dam wall was eventually undermined and collapsed. The question of negligence was again raised but no legal action was taken against the Water Board or any of the Engineers concerned. Once again it seems that the engineering expertise required to build such enormous structures was lacking. The Sheffield Flood remains the UK's major civil catastrophe of the Victorian era.

The concluding statement of the Government Inspector, Captain Moody, was precise and prescient:

'In this neighbourhood there are many mountain reservoirs receiving floods of waters, impounded by lofty dams; pray don't look upon them and treat them like mill-dams or fish-ponds. They are engines of mighty force, strong in aid of your industry to augment your wealth, and terrible in their power to destroy if mismanaged or neglected. The fact must be indelibly impressed on the minds of all the dwellers in Holmfirth.'

If only Sheffield had heeded this warning!

THE FORGOTTEN FLOOD OF 1944

CHAPTER 7

WHIT MONDAY, 1944

Monday, 29th May, 1944 dawned sunny and bright, but with just a hint of rain to come. The weather had been unsettled for a few days, but it was warm. One witness spoke of it as the hottest day of the year so far. It seemed to be typical May weather; later it turned out to be anything but typical.

In the early afternoon the atmosphere was said to be hot, stuffy and electrical, with black clouds over Holme Moss. A few heavy but scattered showers fell on the high moors and lightning intensity increased. One witness talked of feeling encircled by the weather, with a sulphurous taste in the air. The rain started in earnest at around 5 o'clock, and moved slowly down the valley.

Monday, 29th May, 1944, was also Whitsuntide and a Bank Holiday. This Bank Holiday has now been secularised and is called the Spring Bank Holiday, replacing the movable feast of Whitsuntide. The holiday had been anticipated for some time. The usual Whit Monday activities were being planned and many townsfolk were involved, especially the Sunday School Children. Whit Monday was the occasion of the Sunday School Festival, the sing, an event which had been celebrated for over 100 years.

The Sing, similar to this one, was being held in Victoria Park. This would luckily draw people away from the town centre and the destructive river.

All the Churches combined their Sunday Schools for this annual feast. The local park on the hill, Victoria Park, was reserved for the occasion. The Park provided a natural amphitheatre, with stepped seating or standing places round a level area. The schoolchildren would stand or sit ranged across the hillside, round the band (or more usually bands, for they also combined for the occasion). A podium would be erected for the conductor and for the Minister to give his address.

The Park was the culmination of the events of the day. The Sunday School children would parade from their respective Churches, young and old together, with banners flying and bands playing. They would often stop at appropriate places to sing a hymn, before moving on to the Park. There would be considerable rivalry between the Sunday Schools - usually of the more friendly variety.

If wet, the proceedings would be abandoned and revert to the largest Church Hall for games. Tea would be provided in any case and each child, with luck, would take home a sticky bun. But only if wet..... Many observers have noted that the presence of so many children and parents in the park reduced the death toll. If they had not been there, many would have been down by the riverside, right in the line of the flood.

There were other activities, of course. There was a cricket match, a local derby with Honley, from four kilometres down the valley. The teams were made up of the young and enthusiastic, or the old and experienced, with little in between. The local cinema, the Valley Theatre, was putting on a 'Colossal Attraction for Whitsun' for the afternoon and evening. "The Bells Go Down", a comedy starring Tommy Trinder, was the special film for the occasion, supported by Shirley Temple in "Miss Annie Rooney". It was all calculated to provide as much cheer as was practical.

For many there was simply the chance to stroll around and meet friends, in a welcome break from everyday wartime activities. For the more energetic, a longer hike over the mountains, with drinks and sandwiches, was eagerly anticipated. The high moors that day were crowded with enthusiastic hikers, taking advantage of the good weather and the short break.

Over all these events, however, there was a shadow, a shadow not at all connected with the weather. The whole country was waiting, anxiously but with hope, for the impending invasion of the mainland of Europe by combined British and American forces, with assistance from our other allies.

Everyone knew that this was being planned, because so many people were involved in it. But only a favoured few knew where the invasion was to be launched and no one knew exactly when it would occur. This would ultimately depend on the weather, although many other factors had to be taken into account.

The wartime situation meant that local festivities would be subdued. Most of the able bodied menfolk were away and had been for some years. For many there would be more years of absence and separation. Some of them would never come back. There was therefore something of an enforced air of enjoyment about the proceedings. All the usual activities were being pursued, but without the usual enthusiasm.

Sh-sh-h-h!

The Germans are desperately anxious for any scrap of information about our invasion plans. An odd word, unwarily spoken, may give to listening ears the clue to a whole operation. Now, more than ever before, careless talk is dangerous. It may cost thousands of lives and delay victory for months.

What do I do...?

I remember that what seems common knowledge to me may be valuable news to the enemy.

I never discuss troop movements or ship's sailings or convoys I have seen on the road.

I never talk about my war-work or the position of factories or deliveries of war material.

I keep a special guard on my tongue in public places — in parks, pubs, uses restaurants, railway stations and trains, and when talking on the 'phone.

Whatever I see, learn, or happen to know *I keep it to myself.*

Issued by the Ministry of Information

ace presented to the Nation by the Brewers' Society

Wartime security, an advertisement from the Holmfirth Express

Wartime savings were actively encouraged, with an almost poetic touch

There is always someone

fiercely reminding

those who fight

—though not in words—

"Do not relax!"

That someone

is the enemy.

And that message

is also for us in Britain.

It is stern reality

that says SALUTE

THE FIGHTING FORCES

with more

and yet more saving!

National wartime events had another effect. The flood took place a few days before the invasion of Europe and a news blackout was in force. News was not censored, but it was controlled and managed. Mail to and from the soldiers was delayed, so that secrecy was maintained. No information of potential use to the enemy was to be allowed out and no information which might undermine morale was allowed in. The motto 'Sh sh h h - keep it dark' became a wartime catchphrase and newspaper advertisements, warning of careless talk, were regularly published.

Similarly stories in the newspapers were controlled and news of the flood in Holmfirth was delayed. No account of it was allowed to be published in any newspaper for 10 days. By the time publication was permitted the invasion of Europe was underway and belated news of a relatively minor flood was no longer news. The local weekly paper, the 'Holmfirth Express' (now the 'Holme Valley Express') was able to publish details on the 3rd, 10th and 17th June. Wartime restrictions on paper limited the issues to one piece of folded broadsheet - four pages to contain all the details of a monumental event for the Holme Valley.

The Huddersfield Daily Examiner explained 'In order that the enemy may not be helped to forecast the weather by knowing what is taking place over Britain, no mention may be publicly made of metrological conditions or happenings except in the Straights of Dover until 10 days have elapsed.' The story in this paper, headed 'A Shocking River Mishap' gave due non-prominence to the event.

As a consequence the story of the flood was largely overlooked, except for the suffering inhabitants of Holmfirth. Even today, the story of the Holmfirth Flood remains a forgotten flood outside the local area.

It turned out to be the hottest day of the year so far. Although rain clouds built up during the afternoon, there was relatively little rain, in short and fitful showers, in Holmfirth itself. The cricket match was played in between the showers, until it was finally rained off, abandoned after Honley had completed their innings and scored 86.

The local Methodist Minister, Rev R A Blackburn, was just beginning his address to the Sunday School Sing, in the Park, at about 6 o'clock. This point saw the onset of another heavy shower, which finally persuaded the organisers to put into effect Plan B and adjourn the activities into the Church Hall. Mr Blackburn must surely have been disappointed at being deprived of the opportunity of delivering an address of prophetic quality, entitled 'The Power of Water'.

The main rainfall, a cloudburst, took place higher up the valley, on the moors surrounding Bilberry Reservoir (the scene, coincidentally, of the 1852 Flood). On the moors the downpour was described as like a thick mist, with rain falling and swirling, it seemed, in all directions. It was a sudden, massive fall of rain and most of it drained quickly off into one small valley, causing a flash flood which scoured a trail of devastation for five kilometres down the valley, with effects far wider afield.

Where to get your new Ration Book

Consumers who have not yet applied for
their New Ration Books may obtain them
.at

HOLMFIRTH FOOD OFFICE

during ordinary office hours, as follows:

9 a.m. to 5-30 p.m.

Saturdays. 9 a.m. to 12 noon.

WHAT TO DO *before you go to the Distribution Office*

1 Your Identity Card must be signed with your name on the inside in the space
marked "Holder's Signature." It should also have your present permanent
address on it. If it has not, or if you have lost your card, go at once to your
local National Registration Office (same address as the Food Office), taking your
present Ration Book with you. Remember, it's no use going to a Ration Book
distribution office if your Identity Card is lost or incorrect.

2 Page 3 of your PRESENT RATION BOOK has been left blank so far. This
must be filled in now. (The page is not to be cut out.) Then, on page 36 of your
present Ration Book, make sure that the names and addresses of your retailers
are written or stamped in the spaces provided.

Note : Take your Identity Card and present Ration Book with you when you go
to get your new Book. If you are getting anyone else's Book, take his or her Identity
Card and Ration Book properly filled in, too.

If you are an expectant mother and are due to go to the Food Office between May 22nd
and July 23rd to get your Green Ration Book renewed, you can get your new Ration
Books at the same time and so save yourself a second journey. Holders of temporary (yellow) Identity Cards who have to apply for extension during this period
can also get their Ration Books at the same time.

*Food Facts will tell you what to do
after you get your new Ration Book*

MINISTRY OF FOOD

Everything was in short supply, or rationed. Everybody had to have a Ration Book from the
Ministry of Food

43

CHAPTER 8

CLOUDBURST ON THE MOORS

At first, there was surprisingly little rain in Holmfirth; just the usual scattered showers which are a feature, as everyone knows, of an English Bank Holiday. However, five kilometres to the west, where the mass of the Pennine range rises to a height of over 1800 feet, a huge black cloud hovered. It could be seen miles away. A lady in Keighley, whose home was in Hinchliffe Mill, saw the cloud and commented to a friend that 'someone was in for a lot of rain'. How right she was! The floor of her own home was covered in a layer of mud.

There were many eye witnesses to the weather on that day. Mr Frank Booth, watching from Hillhouse, Cartworth Moor, had a panoramic view over a wide area of the moor, stretching from Holme Moss to the Isle of Skye public house (now no more) high up on the Greenfield road. His account vividly describes the cloudburst from his vantage point.

'At 5.05 in the afternoon, a thick mist could be seen spreading from the village of Holme, and a black vertical cloud wall was at the entrance to Digley valley. It was like a meteorological cold front - a bank of hot atmosphere meeting cold air and walling vertically up. The progress of the storm could be seen through Holmbridge and down the valley, but the black bank of cloud remained, blotting out Digley valley.

'At 5.25 the horizon from Holme Moss to the Isle of Skye was bright orange as if the moors were on fire. As the storm cloud rose higher, this belt of colour increased and changed to a nasty blue, and then to a dull grey. Eventually visibility increased up the Digley valley. First the cricket field appeared, covered with yellow mud, and later Bilberry reservoir.

'The heightened water level was obvious, and flows of water could be seen running out at either side of the embankment and meeting in the middle at its foot, with no water coming over the embankment itself. There was more lightning and a strong gale sprang up. Water was gushing down the valley at a great depth.

'Three large, black twisted columns could be seen, with the reverse effect of white rays of sunlight through cloud, coming to ground at Digley, Hinchliffe Mill and Hillhouse. The third column was a solid thunderspout, 100

44

feet wide, composed of intense drops driven at high
velocity by the wind. Water was running down the road and
fields, two feet deep in a matter of seconds.

'From 6.25 to 7 o'clock the storm was at its height.
Roaring and crashing could be heard from the mills. Many
buildings seemed to be struck by multiple streaks of
lightning converging just above them and coming down with
a whistle and sharp crack like a whiplash, followed by
huge thunderclaps. As the water came down, many of the
mill buildings seemed to shiver and gave the effect of a
man trying to get out from under a tarpaulin sheet. The
heavy rain lasted until 8 o'clock.'

The rain clouds had built up over the southern counties and moved north until, near
Sheffield, weathermen observed that a huge pile of cumulo-nimbus clouds had
collected. It looked like an enormous cauliflower about 25,000 feet in height. It was
also noted, with some concern, that the cloud had become unstable. It eventually burst
over the South Yorkshire/North Derbyshire Pennines.

Another witness, Katherine Lockwood, was out on a hike with her parents and they had
stopped to rest at Ramsden Reservoir. She describes a cloud over Holme village,
circular in shape, which seemed to move in a circle, increasing in size and getting
darker and darker. There was some thunder around 2.30 and some rain. When they
reached the village centre, Miss Battye, on the village green, asked them into her house
for shelter, with typical Yorkshire hospitality. Inside the house at the height of the
storm, a strong wind was blowing the rain almost horizontally and it seemed as if
someone was throwing buckets of water at the windows. The lightning was almost
continuous, in brilliant purple flashes and very frightening. When the rain had stopped,
they walked towards Digley valley and noted that the track was covered in debris
washed from the fields, including stones and potatoes.

Aileen Brook was one of a foursome on a Whit Monday hike. As they approached
Holme village they noticed a vivid flash of lightning, which lit up the valley with a
ghostly, bluish-white light. What surprised them most was that they were looking down
on to the lightning, down in the valley.

The cloudburst, when it eventually came that evening, was both heavy and prolonged.
The Waterworks Manager to Huddersfield Corporation estimated that three to four
inches (8 to 10 cm) of rain fell in an hour and a half. Some areas had a particular
concentration of rainfall. It was estimated that about five inches (12 cm) fell near
Bilberry Reservoir, whereas at Yateholme Reservoir, only two miles away, 1.66 inches
(4 cm) were recorded.

It fell over a wide area of the Pennines of South Yorkshire, and over the moors in North
Derbyshire, near Glossop. The downpour was too sudden and heavy to be absorbed in
the ground and it flowed downhill, with devastating swiftness, mainly into the Holme
Valley. The rain from a wide area was channelled into a narrow valley, the watercourse

of the River Holme. The town of Glossop on the Derbyshire side of the mountain also suffered damage because of the flood.

Bilberry Reservoir, which burst to cause the 1852 flood, had been rebuilt on a smaller scale. Just before the rain came, the water level in the Reservoir was 12 feet (3.5 metres) below its maximum. The first 25 million gallons that fell in the catchment area filled up this space, and then overflowed at both ends of the embankment. If this volume of water had not been constrained, the effects further down the valley would have been even more horrific.

The dam wall held, but the overspill down the valley was too fierce to be contained, and yards of the riverbank, about 100 tons, was washed away. Much of the downpour was outside the dam catchment area, and flowed straight down the hillside streams to swell the flow.

The ruins of Digley Mill, showing how the river had changed it's course. The mill was disused and had been demolished at the time of the flood, although the mill chimney was still standing. All this scene is now covered by Digley Reservoir, with the dam wall built approximately where the road runs across the picture.

The course of the river went through the sites of the old mills in the Digley valley, which had ceased operations some years earlier. Digley Mill was the most recent, having closed down in 1938. The buildings and cottages attaching to it had been demolished, except for the tall square chimney and some derelict outbuildings. The old cottage gardens were overgrown, although enterprising visitors could, at the right time of the year, find a surprising quantity of wild raspberries, to go with the bilberries and blackberries which were the usual crop in the area.

The ongoing rush of water made short work of all this. The river burst its shallow banks, flooding over the sites of the mills, uprooting most of the plants in the garden and undermining the road. By the time the waters had subsided, the course of the river had been changed. The chimney and outbuildings survived, a tribute to the strength of the stonework of the Victorian builders.

Luckily, no one lived at that point of valley floor, so no lives were lost and no homes destroyed. However, such a weight of water still had power to damage, as the people down the valley would soon find out. The cricket field in Holmbridge was the first to suffer, as ten feet (three metres) were eroded off the square leg boundary. The green grass of the cricket field was covered in a layer of brown mud - like a gigantic chocolate cake, observed Edward Hinchliffe.

Stumpit Lane (a corruption of Stone Pit Lane) is about a quarter of a mile (400 metres) upstream from Holmbridge church. It is, as the name implies, a narrow and stoney footpath, running down from Field End Lane into Digley Lane in the valley bottom. Mrs Ruth Mary Beardsell was watching as the rainwater flowed down, turning the rocky and steep footpath into a rocky and swiftly moving stream. The water rushed down the path and across to a row of cottages (now demolished) where she lived. She was surprised to find that the water had sped through Grandad Hinchliffe's cottage on the same row and carried away his dinner, still in a roasting tin.

The bridge and buildings at Holmbridge were next in the line of destruction. The parapet of the bridge was washed away with the force of the water and the houses at the bottom of Holme Bank were flooded. Alderson's cafe, a large prefabricated wooden structure, was rocked on its foundations, but held firm.

Edward Hinchliffe had arrived in Holmbridge on the last bus from Huddersfield, before the road was washed away. As an eight year old boy he remembers clearly arriving at the Church in Holmbridge, where the rainstorm was so heavy that the bus could not turn round as usual. The driver moved it on, above the level of the water, whilst his passengers, all six of them, sheltered inside.

Two buses were stranded at Holmbridge and eventually had to make their way back to their depot on the hill road via Woodhouse Quarry and Cook's Study and then down Scholes Moor Road back to Huddersfield.

The fury of the water was turned against the buildings of Holme Bridge mill, owned by W H and J Barber. Between the mill buildings was the confluence of two rivers; Digley stream, coming from Digley, and the main River Holme flowing down the valley from Ramsden and Brownhill, with its four back up reservoirs. Both streams were swollen with the cloudburst and they met, in raging foam, between the mill buildings.

The enforced merging of two streams pushed the water level up so high that much of the riverbank was eroded and a corner of the mill warehouse was undermined. Some of the stock of the mill, huge bales of wool, fell in and added to the destruction. The water rose to cover the floor of the Parish Hall and adjoining houses, leaving behind a layer of filthy, smelly ouse. Many people in Holmbridge (and all down the valley) commented

The road damage to the bridge on Ford Road/Dobb Lane, Hinchliffe Mill, looking downstream towards Holmfirth. The arch, built around 1838 has survived the force of both the 1852 devastation as well as the 1944 flood.

The same bridge at Hinchliffe Mill, looking up Dobb Lane. The eroded road surface is clearly visible. At some stage the bridge was widened and the arch of the original bridge wss hidden by the straight beam.

on the unpleasant smell which followed the floodwaters.

Further down the valley, the river flowed round and across the sports field and then into a narrow ravine. This constricted the water, raising the level and increasing the force of the flow. Normally the river would be no more than a foot deep, with stones worn smooth by the action of the water over the centuries. Now the water level rose to ten or twelve feet (3 to 4 metres), and sped downhill with increasing ferocity.

On Ford Gate, Hinchliffe Mill, the river met its next barrier, in the shape of the road bridge on Dobb Lane. It was here that the bales of wool jammed under the bridge, and formed a dam behind which the water rose even higher. The houses on Ford Gate and Water Lane are normally well above the water level. Now the waters were forced up until they covered the ground floor, to a depth of several feet in some cases. The sandbags which had been hastily laid on the flagstones of each doorway were completely ineffective in keeping the water at bay. The level of water in the river spreading into the mill dam made it look like one big reservoir.

On its way down, the river had picked up more debris, as well as the bales of wool. Henhouses built near the river were soon floated from their foundations, and began their journey down the rapids. Betty Hobson, looking out from the window of no. 46 Ford Gate, was somewhat surprised to see one shed float majestically past the window of her front room. It was only one event in a day full of shocks and surprises.

Amongst the debris washed down by the water were a few sheep, drowned in the downpour and dye from the dyeworks. In places cows were marooned, lost and bedraggled as their fields were submerged.

The woolbale barrier was only temporary and the water flowed round, over the river bank and road bridge, taking with it the parapet and much of the roadway. The walls alongside the river, built of dry stone walling, were already collapsing into piles of rubble, but were too heavy to move far downriver.

Mrs Greensmith, at no 26, was looking out of her window and watching her outside toilet across the road, alongside the river. The primitive Yorkshire builders had taken full advantage of the natural resources of the river when they chose the site. She watched in horror as it was undermined and collapsed into the water to be flushed away for ever.

Mrs Audrey Helm, who remembers stories from her grandfather about the Great Flood in Holmfirth, also recalls her uncle, Fletcher Parson, and his stories of the 1944 flood in his house on Water Street. She also had other aunts and uncles, in two households, luckily just above the flood waters at Prickleden. It is amazing that there are still families with living memories covering both floods; a tribute to the longevity of valley folk.

A few yards further downstream the river ran alongside the tall buildings of Whiteley and Green's mill. The wall of the finishing room was undermined, being built over the river, and machinery and goods were washed downstream. One machine, weighing some six to eight tons, finished up 200 yards (180 metres) downriver. Further down still the flood continued past Bottoms Mill, owned by T & J Tinker, eroding parts of the riverbank on its way. A clock in the mill was stopped at 6.20.

At this point the river changed course again, and cut through the premises of R H Dark & Co Ltd. This was third time unlucky for R H Dark. In October, 1940, they had been bombed out of their original premises in London; then, after transferring to a factory in the Holme Valley, they had suffered extensive damage by gales. Now the floodwater carried away 400 expensive bales of rabbit wool and skins, each weighing between a quarter and a half a ton and with a value at the time of about £15,000.

Silvia Lee was looking down the hill from her home at Malkin House, when she saw the two reservoirs at Perseverance Mill (now demolished, but situated opposite the Victoria Inn) merge into one and flood through the mill.

The river surged through the Victoria Ironworks, belonging to W W Battye & Sons Ltd, and deposited quantities of mud all over the ground floor of the premises. Small tools and stock were rendered unuseable. The clock in the factory stopped at 6.25.

It was here that two of the three fatalities occurred. Miss Maude Evelyn Wimpenny, aged 76, lived by herself on the track leading down to the Victoria Ironworks. Her house was below the level of the road, and her ground floor quickly became submerged as the waters in the river rose. She managed to struggle out of her house and took refuge kneeling on a wall in front of an adjoining house. A neighbour, Mr Donald Riley, was with his 14 year old son Geoffrey, and saw Miss Wimpenny in difficulties on the wall.

Geoffrey's statement at the inquest tells us what happened.

> 'At about half past six I was with my father at the bottom of Victoria Dam bank when I saw Miss Wimpenny on the wall near her home, between her house and the river. We rushed down the road and got a clothes line from a house on the main road. I got on to a wall and tried to throw the rope to her, but was unable to do so. Dad shouted at me to go back. I took off my clothes and went into the water.
>
> I was able to stand in the water, which was up to my waist. I got Miss Wimpenny off the wall and part of the way back. The water had got a bit deeper by then and there was a strong current, but it did not wash me off my feet. The water was washing us towards the river bank. I heard my Dad shout "Hang on, Lad", and he came in and reaching me, he got hold of me with one hand and hold of the wall with the other. Then the wall collapsed. We were all washed into the river.
>
> 'I was carried some distance down the river, then I got on to a hen hut roof which was floating in the water and someone threw me a hose pipe off a stirrup pump. I managed to get hold of that and I was pulled out, but I never saw my Dad and Miss Wimpenny again.'

Miss Wimpenny and Mr Riley were swept away and drowned. Geoffrey was pulled out of the river near the Valley Dyeworks. 'I shan't see my Dad again,' he told Mr and Mrs Willie Battye, who had rescued him from the raging waters.

The body of Miss Wimpenny was carried down river and was eventually found lodged under a mill skip in the mud and debris at Lower Mill. The body of Mr Riley was found at 9.15 that evening, at the far side of Holmfirth, beyond Mytholmbridge, where two stay wires across the river had trapped him, along with debris from the flood.

The District Coroner, Mr E W Norris paid tribute to the bravery of Geoffrey Riley at the inquest, held at the Holme Valley Memorial Hospital. 'I understand that the bravery of Geoffrey Riley has already been mentioned and appreciated in the District, but I should like to say he acted in an extremely plucky manner. It is sad that he lost his father

through this fatality.'
The London Gazette of 3rd October, 1944, had the following announcement:

'The KING has been pleased to award the Albert Medal to
Geoffrey Riley in recognition of his gallantry.' The
citation concluded 'He (Geoffrey Riley) then entered
the flood water, rescued her from the wall which later
collapsed, and though only a moderate swimmer,
struggled to bring her to safety through the flood until
he became exhausted. His father, Donald Riley, went to
his assistance, but all three were swept away into the
river, Geoffrey Riley being the sole survivor.'

The Albert Medal was subsequently converted to the George Medal, and the original
Albert Medal can now be found in the Tolson Museum at Ravensknowle Park,
Huddersfield..

CHAPTER 9

THE FLOOD IN HOLMFIRTH TOWN CENTRE

At the Victoria public house the river swings sharply to the right and runs alongside the road. In May, 1944, the river had a mind of its own and tried to carve a new watercourse under the highway. A huge gap was opened up in the road, and twenty yards (18 metres) of wall with most of the road was washed away. Huddersfield Corporation electricity and gas pipes were severed, as were Batley corporation water pipes, thus ironically adding to the force of water downstream. The road was to remain unusable for months, as the retaining wall had to be rebuilt from the foundations.

The road undermined and washed away by the Victoria Inn, showing broken gas and water pipes. It took several months to make the road useable again.

The destructive force swept away the parapets of the bridge to Perseverance Mill and continued towards Holmfirth. The rushing debris damaged the premises of the Valley Dyeworks.

Nearer the town centre stands Lower Mill (owned by H & S Butterworth) strategically placed at a bend in the river and at the entrance to a narrowing of the valley at Scarfold. Lower Mill was built over the river, and provided a barrier against which more bales of wool and debris lodged. This effectively dammed up the river and the water level rose and overflowed the roof of the weaving shed. The power of the water pushed in the walls, crumpled the roof supports and left machinery bent and twisted. It is likely that this saved the centre of the town from more severe damage. The dam of bales sapped some of the force from the pent up water and afforded a small measure of protection for the town centre.

The damage at lower mill, just as the river runs into Scarfold. The river here was chocked with bales of wool, which diverted the flood waters through the single story mill buildings. The mill in the background has since been demolished.

The flood waters surged past Scarfold, where the narrow valley helped to push up the levels even higher. Any bales of wool and other debris in the water acted like battering rams hitting Upperbridge, sweeping away the parapet and completely overwhelming the walls alongside Hollowgate. The road is very low lying at this point, and was soon covered in about twelve feet (3.5 metres) of water. At one stage the river was eighteen feet (5.5 metres) above its normal level.

At the height of the flood in Victoria Square, looking up Hollowgate, with Rotcher on the left of the picture.

At the height of the flood in Hollowgate, taken from around the Elephant and Castle pub and looking towards Victoria Square. The buildings on the left was Castle's Garage. This has since been refurbished as the Holmfirth Mill Shop.

A car from Castle's Garage is washed away.

The houses on the riverbank at Scarfold are underdwellings of property at Upperbridge opening on to Huddersfield Road. The river rose almost to the level of the first floor of the underdwellings and trapped worried inhabitants on the upper floor. Councillor Tolson put his head out of a window of one of the houses above, and saw Mr and Mrs Barratt, a retired couple, trapped in the house below. With a crowbar Councillor Tolson prized up a flagstone in the floor of the sitting room, then used a pickaxe to make a hole in the ceiling of the Barratt's bedroom. A step ladder was lowered to the stranded

Hollowgate after the waters have subsided.

inhabitants who then climbed through their ceilings to the floor above.

The same procedure had to be followed to rescue Miss Lydia Schofield and then Mr and Mrs Wilfred Maxfield from adjoining houses into the houses at Upperbridge of Miss Sykes and Miss Battye. All the people thus rescued were described as 'elderly'. Many of them were accommodated for the night at the home of Mr J Collins, who had an enlarged household of sixteen.

One ARP warden hurriedly put on his greatcoat and rushed down to the town centre to see what help he could give. On passing the Elephant and Castle pub he fell through the trapdoor to the cellar, where the water had washed away the wooden cover. Luckily his greatcoat kept him afloat until he was pulled out.

The damage caused by the high and fast flowing water spread all the way through the town centre. All the ground floors were flooded along Hollowgate and at least two residents had to be rescued by ladder from the upstairs windows. Mr Herbert Senior had watched the waters rise, but had not appreciated their ferocity. Elsewhere Mr Willie Sykes was asleep and was unaware of the flood. Buildings on the riverbank at Hollowgate were under the greatest threat and several collapsed.

The rescue of Willie Sykes, asleep on the first floor of his underdwelling on Hollowgate, was particularly dramatic. Above Mr Sykes' house was a store room belonging to Mr Quarmby and opening on to a lane off Rocher. The rescuers entered this store room, and lowered a ladder from the store room to Mr Sykes' bedroom. Constable Fearns tied a rope around his waist, descended the ladder and smashed through the window of the bedroom. He tied a rope around Mr Sykes and the two of them ascended the ladder, which was being held in position from above.

Both the garage of GW Castle Ltd and Baddeley's Buses were built on Huddersfield Road, but had newly built bridges at the rear over the river to Hollowgate. Both bridges were swamped, and much damage was done, especially to vehicles. One vehicle was swept down Hollowgate, manoeuvred through the narrow ginnel behind Martins Bank (now Barclays Bank) and deposited in The Nook, on the bed of the River Ribble just outside the Rose and Crown pub. Next morning its lights were still on.

The bridge to Arthur Quarmby's slaughterhouse, and the business premises along Hollowgate, all suffered; F & F J Marsden, builders and contractors, and the shops owned by D H Howard, L Green, Brook Turner and George Mason & Son.

The properties at the bottom of Victoria Street felt the full force of the flood. The river undermined Wallace's the grocer and then Mrs Lillian Torr's millinery shop, and both dropped into the water in a cloud of grey dust. A few moments later the same fate happened to the offices of the Huddersfield Building Society. On Hollowgate the premises of the Prudential Assurance Company and the Yorkshire Penny Bank, together with the offices of Mr P N Brown, the architect, were destroyed. These buildings also included some homes on the upper floors.

Other properties which suffered damage included some businesses still in being today: the butchers shop of Arthur Quarmby on one side of the river, and his home on the other; and Mr J W Kaye, Ironmongers. Other businesses were Mr Walter Quarmby, Gents Outfitters, Mr W Haigh, Chemist, Mr H Teasdeall and Mr G H Smith (both butchers) and Mr Cartwright's general outfitter store.

The pubs in the village centre were damaged. The worst damage was to the Elephant and Castle, alongside Upperbridge, but the King's Head, the Shoulder of Mutton and the White Hart also suffered. The Rose and Crown, hidden in The Nook behind Martins Bank, was flooded to a depth of three or four feet (about one metre), washing over a piano in the process.

The wide roadway of Victoria Square was soon covered to a depth of three feet (one metre). A strong cross current swept round The Nook from both directions and met in front of the Rose and Crown. The swirling water trapped LAC Stanley Turton (on leave from the Royal Air Force), who had to climb 20 feet (6 metres) up a fallpipe on to the rooftops. He was rescued by ladder when the river subsided.

The water flowed down Market Walk, a promenade built over the river and leading to the Valley Theatre and threatened to bring down the entrance. Inside the Theatre, the projectionist, Mr H Hopkins, noticed the rising waters and called a halt to the film. He asked the public, calmly and quietly, to leave by the back entrance. This was carried out without fuss and 300 cinemagoers were taken to safety.

Unfortunately, those on the balcony had no such means of escape. They had to wait for the fire brigade to bring in ladders so that they could climb down to safety. Meanwhile, the promenade in front of the Theatre had collapsed into the engorged river.

In Towngate properties were flooded, including Mr H Battye's, the tailors, the Boot and Shoe Society's store and Mr A Woodhead's. It was here that the third fatality occurred, when Mrs Dorothea Schofield was drowned. She was employed by Baddeleys Bros at their garage on Towngate and was in control of the taxis of the business.

A witness at the Inquest, Lewis Hirst, told his story. He had come from Huddersfield with his taxi, to seek further instructions. He had come through a terrific rainstorm between Honley and Holmfirth, but did not notice the river in flood at the bottom of Victoria Street. As he tried to leave, he could not get his taxi to start because of water in the engine. He continued:

'Mrs Schofield came down to see what was wrong, and we were there for approximately ten minutes trying to start it. Then Mrs Schofield went back into the house for the garage key, and I pushed the car into the garage yard, which contained no water at that time. Mrs Schofield was about to unlock the garage door when the flood water came through the garage yard gate.

'I asked her to get into the car to escape getting wet. She got in the front seat and I was in the driving seat. The water rose rapidly and I assisted her out to comparatively dry ground. We made our way to the wall between the garage yard and the main road and walked along it for about 15 yards, with the intention of getting into Station Road, where the ground was higher.

'We climbed on to the top of the wall, but found it impossible to get across the road owing to the rush of water. We had to get on to a higher wall because of the rapid rise of the water. We tried to reach the top of the air raid shelter in the garage yard, but the wall between us and the shelter was washed away. The water came through the gate in one wave. We should have been safe if we had got into a bus in the mill yard.

'We returned to our original position on the higher wall. After we had been there for about eight minutes the wall collapsed. We were both washed into the river. I lost sight of Mrs Schofield immediately. I was washed down the river for some distance and then managed to cling to a bale of yarn bobbins. From that position I was rescued.'

A horrified crowd watched from a distance, powerless to help. Mr Hirst's mother was watching. He implored her to go away, but even as they watched the wall collapsed and

Collapse of Market Walk

Victoria Bridge

the couple were cast into the water.

Mrs Schofield's body was found at 8.15 that evening, entangled in a tree jutting out from the bank, about 150 yards (135 metres) from the Technical Institute.

The force of the water was abating a little as it spread out over a wider area. The river flowed through a small area clear of buildings and continued down the valley. It still carried along its burden of debris, but most of the heavy bales of wool had been left behind. By the time the river flowed past the cricket field it was deep but had done most of its destructive work.

The high water swept on down the valley, past Thongsbridge, Brockholes and Honley, carrying with it flotsam and jetsam which it had picked up on its journey through Holmfirth. Some debris was found as far away as Dewsbury and Horbury, near Wakefield.

At Brockholes there was still sufficient strength in the river flow to maroon Miss Maggie Hallas at her poultry run at the bottom of Smithy Place Lane. Mr R Richardson tried unsuccessfully to rescue her twice and eventually the National Fire Service had to be summoned.

Although the water left behind a trail of damage, it was only a flash flood, a huge wave which swept down the valley. The level of the water rose and fell within less than an hour, when all the damage was done. If the water had been delayed or regulated by some means, it could have flowed down the proper watercourses without any problem: it does every year, at times of heavy rain. However, on very rare occasions, perhaps once every century, a huge cloudburst occurs to show us that even a placid and peaceful stream like the River Holme can have a fiercer and more destructive nature.

CHAPTER 10

THE AFTERMATH

Even after the floodwaters had subsided, the area was still liable to further flooding from reservoirs overfull of water and with weakened embankments and blocked overflow channels. The National Fire Service (NFS) were pumping water from the Bilberry reservoir throughout Tuesday, and reduced the level by 7 inches (about 17 cm), but an hour of rain on Wednesday filled it up again.

On Wednesday, two days after the flood, it was felt that the potential for further flooding was so great that an alarm system was required. A telephone line was run from Bilberry to Bottoms Mill, and the Police obtained special permission for the siren at the mill to be sounded, not as an Air Raid warning but as a flood warning. Loudspeaker vans would tour the area to reinforce the warning. If the siren sounded, all of the low lying parts of Holmfirth would have to be evacuated, to avoid a repetition of the 1852 disaster.

In the event, the water rose to within a quarter of an inch (6 mm) of the danger level, and for a few hours it was touch and go as to whether the valley would need to be evacuated. Watch was kept on the embankment, day and night, for four days before the water level was thought to be sufficiently low to be no further danger. Few people at the time realised how close the valley was to an emergency evacuation.

Although the flood was of such short duration, the damage it caused was immense. The country had grown used to damage, because after nearly five years of war ruined cities and buildings were continually in the news. Many other cities and towns had suffered far worse devastation and over a longer period. In the South of England, where many of Holmfirth's inhabitants were employed in preparation for the invasion, there were many buildings suddenly and ferociously destroyed. Thousands of Londoners and other citizens had suffered far more in death, destruction and injury.

There were already civilian and military organisations in place to take control for war damage and the same facilities were immediately available for the assistance of those suffering from the destruction caused by the flood. The Civil Defence functioned smoothly to meet the disaster, and were able to summon reinforcements from many surrounding areas. The Regional Mobile Column rendered yeoman service in the clearing of the river bed of obstacles and debris and the restoration of the river to its original course. They removed the bales of material from Lower Mill and other mills where they were considered to be a menace to public health or safety.

Commencing on Tuesday, the Civil Defence and other services were engaged on the cleansing of premises by pumping, digging, scouring and mopping. In all over 100 premises were dealt with. The work was rendered more difficult by the fairly constant rain over the following days. The work in connection with the cleansing of private premises was organized by the Wardens and Rescue Parties and it is worthy of note that these people worked all day on Whit Tuesday and the following Sunday and in the evening of every other day in addition to Saturday afternoon. The National Fire Service pumped out all the cellars of the private houses and business premises affected.

At one time as many as 700 Air Raid Wardens, rescue teams, messengers, Home Guard and Special Constables were co-operating with the National Fire Service and the regular police. A Unit of the American Army was stationed in nearby Penistone and they readily loaned men and machines to assist in the task of clearing up and making the area safe and habitable. Even Italian prisoners of war helped in the repair of the damaged wall.

Proper communications were required to meet the flood emergency. Loud speaker vans were borrowed from the Police and from Mr H G Heaton of Honley and were very effective. Their first use was to call all Civil Defence workers to report to their stations for work and the response was instantaneous. They were used over the following days to give the public reliable and authentic information. In the event no evacuation was necessary because of overflowing reservoirs, but the vans were used to provide the public information about food supplies and potential health hazards.

An emergency rest centre was opened by the Women's Voluntary Service at Lane Congregational Church by 7.30 on the Monday evening. However, by nightfall everyone who had been driven from their homes had found accommodation and hospitality with relatives and friends. Mobile kitchens were brought in to supplement the services of the British Restaurants (the Government run catering organisation). Hot drinks and sandwiches were provided for all those helping to pump out water, clear drains and salvage as much as possible of household furniture and utensils.

The Women's Voluntary Service, the WVS, were at the forefront of this work. A report on their part in the clearing up is a testament to their dedication in overcoming the necessary wartime bureaucracy and in redirecting wartime effort to temporary civilian emergency - even as the invasion plans were coming to a climax.

The Chairman of the local Food Control Committee told them to get some food somehow (without saying how) and the Local Authority would pay for it. Two local shops were able to provide tea, sugar and jam, and the local Co-op bakery was able to supply bread. The local Food Office gave permission to use sugar. The WVS Regional Office provided valuable gifts of sweetened cocoa, dried milk, etc. The Military Welfare Officer sought, and obtained, the use of the YMCA facilities for military use, whilst military facilities were diverted for the civilian emergency.

The WVS ladies were soon hard at work preparing sandwiches to go with the tea. 627 free dinners were served to flood victims and to certain helpers. 8510 cups of tea were dispensed in the first week, rising eventually to a total of 14,000 cups. At a third of a pint per cup, that makes nearly 600 gallons!

The Clothing Officer arranged for clothing from the Emergency Depots to be issued, and the Comforts Committee helped with the distribution. Arrangements were also made for a supply of second hand clothing to be distributed in urgent cases to persons

Local traders publish their thanks for help during the emergency who had lost their clothing. A second hand clothes depot was opened by the Red Cross in the Electricity showrooms. Since wartime rationing applied to clothes as well as food, arrangements had to be made for the replacement of lost clothing coupons.

The Medical Officer was concerned that everyone should have their hands washed in disinfectant before eating and seven buckets were obtained from the Regional Civil Defence Column. These buckets were required to hold disinfectant at each static or mobile canteen. Disinfectant was also sent to each affected house and business premises. The WVS Regional Office provided soap, cleaning materials, brooms and mops, all essential but in short supply.

There was an urgent need to help householders with cleaning carpets, curtains and linen. The Matron of St. Mary's Hospital, Netherthong, provided facilities to clean these domestic fabrics and carpets were spread out in the fields to dry out in the sun.

Although there were piles of stonework and rubble on the low lying streets, this was competently cleared away with the equipment available to the authorities. For most people the main problem arose from clinging, stinking, thick, black mud. It appeared everywhere that the floodwater had immersed. It meant ruination for most of the carpets and furniture covered. As the Council report noted "There is an utter dearth of replacements and the people have not the necessary coupons or permits."

Even a severe Yorkshire scrubbing could not erase the foul odour, compounded of soil, soot, oil, grimes and extracts from wool. Rabbit wool (perhaps an example of wartime expediency) was particularly malodorous. The soot in the water derived from 100 years of chimney sweepings, deposited on riverside gardens to improve garden fertility.

The properties along Hollowgate had suffered particularly badly. All were low lying, and had been covered to a depth of several feet. Every item on the ground floor had to be taken out and cleaned as thoroughly as possible. The woodwork had to be cleaned and allowed to dry out. Cellars, where they existed, had to be pumped dry to get out as much of the odour as possible.

It was a heartbreaking task, but tackled with a grim cheerfulness and determination. 'I never thought I should spend my Whitsuntide holiday doing this', said one girl as she scrubbed away. The work was enlivened by occasional cries of delight when special treasures were found in the mud.

When Bessie Taylor's piano was brought out of her house on Hollowgate it was covered in mud. Nevertheless, once it was cleaned, she greatly enlivened the clearing-up when she sat down at the piano, in the middle of the road, and led the singing of all the popular songs of the day.

Shopkeepers were badly hit. Some premises had been destroyed and much stock was damaged. With wartime shortages, it was not always possible to replace stock. One hardware store lost a recent consignment of washing powder (value £25). One butcher was lucky; his stock was safe in a refrigerator, and he was back in business the following morning, after spending all Monday night clearing the mud from his shop.

The premises of the Yorkshire Penny Bank were destroyed, but the safe was recovered intact. Most of the papers and documents were recovered, undamaged, amongst the rubble. The employees of the fried fish shop were less fortunate; their wage packets had been left on the counter when the flood waters burst in and they were swept away.

Nine factories down the valley were damaged and production was halted. Most of them were able to resume production surprisingly quickly, within two weeks. Others which suffered greater damage managed to have their work transferred to other factories until all the mud had been cleared out and machinery repaired and brought back into service. Few, if any, of the mills were insured against flood, because of the prohibitive cost. The Holme Valley had been designated as a flood area and the insurance rate was "a guinea per cent" (1.05%). One mill estimated that flood insurance would cost £ 750 per annum; multiply that by 30, approximately, for today's cost.

In Hinchliffe Mill, where the houses along Fordgate had suffered inundation (sometimes of only a couple of inches), carpets were taken out and cleaned of as much of the stench as possible. Strong rope was flung over the river and used as a washing line on which the carpets were hung to dry out and freshen up. It was the most convenient place giving sufficient height for the purpose. Later the mill owners kindly allowed their tenter machines to be used to stretch and 'finish' the carpets. Even so, some inhabitants found that their new carpets had shrunk a couple of inches in the process.

High up the valley at Digley, the river had done an efficient job in clearing out the valley floor. The chimney still stood, but otherwise the configuration of the valley had changed beyond recognition. A couple of years later work on the building of the new dam wall of the Digley Reservoir began; by 1952 the valley had been completely transformed.

The roads down the valley were badly affected. The river had swept away bridge parapets and part of the road surface at Holmbridge, Hinchliffe Mill and Upperbridge. The main road at Victoria Square survived well, although in need of remedial work. The main problem was the road at the Victoria Inn, half a mile out of the town on the way up to Holme Moss.

Here the river had vented its full force on the wall which formed the bank of the river and the support for the road. The wall was some twenty feet (six metres) high. The river gouged out a huge piece of the road way, over three quarters of its width. The gas, electric and water supplies were cut. The road had to be closed and all through traffic routed up Greenfield Road, through Parkhead and back down through Burnlee. A footbridge over this minor road at Burnlee meant that only single decker buses could be used along this road until the main road was brought back into service.

The public utility services, cut off at the Victoria Inn (and other places) were speedily if temporarily brought back into service. The electricity supply had been damaged by lightning as well as by the flood and supplies were restored gradually over the next few days. By Monday current was restored to Wooldale and New Mill Road; by Tuesday Shaw Lane and Dunford Road were restored; by Wednesday Rocher, Holmbridge,

Holme and Upperthong were back in service; on Thursday the switch gear at Thongsbridge sub station had been replaced by borrowing equipment from Huddersfield and Halifax; by Friday at 8.30 pm power was restored throughout the district except for the southern side of Victoria Street.

A temporary overground link for gas was restored at the Victoria Inn by midday on Tuesday, 6th June a delay of eight days. At the same time the water supply was connected, overground. The water mains at Victoria were those of Batley Corporation, who had obtained alternative supplies from Dewsbury Corporation. At this time each town was responsible for its own water supply. The sewerage pipeline was laid on the river bed and was broken in several places, allowing raw sewage to flow down the river. However, as the Council noted, the work to survey and repair all this work would be extensive, costly and laborious.

Not all the damaged buildings were rebuilt. The offices of the Huddersfield Building Society and the Yorkshire Penny Bank were not replaced, as it was considered too risky. Other buildings on Hollowgate were repaired, or demolished, to avoid a repetition of similar damage. The promenade built over the river to the Valley Picture Theatre was replaced, in order to give access to the cinema (since closed as a cinema, then a Bingo hall and now reopened as a cinema) and the Conservative Club, now the New Bridge Hotel.

The walls alongside the river throughout its length had to be rebuilt, often from river level. The parapets of all the bridges were repaired, and the roads resurfaced. It is a tribute to the strength of the original bridge builders that after over 100 years they all stood up to the ferocious strength of the river; none needed to be demolished. Yorkshire stone lasts for ever!

One living legacy of the cloudburst has been noted by Edward Hinchliffe. At Bull Clough, a small ravine running down the valley into Brownhill Lane at Holmbridge, all the soil had been washed away, leaving it like a moonscape. Nature somehow contrived to regenerate the area and a forest of silver birch now grows on the site.

Government Assistance for Flood Damage

The civil authorities were full of immediate and practical help in clearing up and rebuilding, but were unable to be as prompt or helpful when it came to replacing stock losses suffered by shopkeepers. The Board of Trade were very sympathetic, but laid their own bureaucratic minefield for official assistance. They had made their own exhaustive enquiries about local consumer needs arising from the flood. Their advice and assistance is recorded below.

```
1.  Retailer's Coupons    (part of the wartime rationing scheme)
    Losses would be made good if the retailers made
    individual application as soon as possible to the
    Board of Trade on form BR/10 (Copies obtainable from
    the Holmfirth Chamber of Trade).
```

2. Stock Replacement. Retailers would have to rely on the goodwill of suppliers, but the Board would be pleased to deal with any difficulties that were reported.

3. Reimbursement of Purchase Tax. Retailers might like to try writing to the Customs and Excise, but the Board of Trade had been in touch with them and it appeared that on no pretext whatever was tax remission given once the point of levy had been passed. Customs and Excise had never departed from the usual procedures

As to other goods:

1. Scrubs, kettles, saucepans, frypans, chambers, babies' chambers, babies' baths and washbowls had been sent to the two principal ironmongers. Existing stocks of buckets and galvanised baths appeared to be adequate. Compassionate supplies of banister and carpet brushes had also been delivered.

2. Supplies of crockery had been found to be equal to the demand, but one sympathetic wholesaler had agreed to forward a special consignment to a local retailer who had suffered flood damage. A small delivery of combs and razor blades had also been directed to two chemists.

3. A quantity of linoleum and coir matter would be directed to the principal retailers as soon as some assessment could be made of the amount likely to be required. The Board were aware that unbacked linoleum was unsuitable for stone floors.

4. People needing new curtain fabrics could obtain a permit enabling them to obtain a limited amount of material by applying to the Board of Trade in London. These permits could be used by retailers to obtain curtain material from their usual suppliers. Stocks of black-out material appeared at present to be adequate.

5. Salvaged goods could be sold at reduced prices and reduced coupon values. Details of the scheme were to be found in paragraph 21 of 'Coupon Quiz', but the

last sub-paragraph concerning war-damaged goods did
not apply.

6. Although victims of flood disaster were not on the
   list of people eligible for Utility furniture, the
   Assistance Board were able at their discretion to
   extend eligibility to the victims of disasters
   other than those caused by enemy action.

7. Emergency supplies of mattresses, blankets and
   pillow cases would be sent to the town if it was
   established that there was a need caused by flood
   damage.

8. The Regional Officer in charge of footwear repairs
   had called that day on shoe repairers in the town,
   offering to assist them in any way.

CHAPTER 11

IN RETROSPECT, SOME LIGHTER MOMENTS

The flood was a serious event, adding a substantial burden to people already greatly concerned for their absent menfolk and continually worried by the progress of the war and the uncertainties of the invasion. The response was a great deal of self help, as already mentioned, so that those flooded out of house and home could soon be satisfactorily resettled.

It was not an easy task to cope with the extra problems, but it was carried out with care and enthusiasm. Underlying it all was a cheerfulness and a dry Yorkshire humour which helped them to cope with their fate. There were certain things which in retrospect seemed ludicrous or amusing.

Oddly enough, someone must have had a premonition of the flood. A correspondent to the Holmfirth Express asked, on 22nd April, five weeks before the flood, "Were there any floods in the Holmfirth District before the disastrous Holmfirth Flood of 1852?"

A list of items observed being carried away by the flood at Honley Bridge, three kilometress downstream from Holmfirth, at 7.30 to 8 o'clock on the evening of the flood were:

20	Cold frames
33	barrels and drums
8	hen huts
1	greenhouse
1	butcher's block
24	trees

numerous garden implements (rakes, brushes, spades)

2	ladders
1	wheelbarrow

house furniture (chairs, stools, tables, a cupboard)

6	cases of beer
100	small tins
1	clothes post
1	tyre
1	lorry jack-board
6	bales,

And 996 planks of wood - (but who counted all these?)

Other novelties observed at Honley included a hen house, still with a white leghorn perched on top - no doubt with a puzzled frown! and a duck, followed by her nest, complete with eggs.

One of the items which was not washed away was a plaque on the wall of a house in Hollowgate - "Don't Worry, it may never happen".

Hen huts and poultry houses figured in many stories of the flood, but one man felt sure that he had the answer. A friend tried to commiserate with him on the loss of his hen house.

The conversation went:

> *"Ah'm sorry, Jack, that tha's lost thi hen 'oil".*
> *"But Ah haven't!"*
> *"Tha has, Ah tell thi."*
> *"Don't be daft. How can Ah have had mi hen 'oil washed away? Ah have the key in mi pocket!"*

(For non Yorkshire speakers, hen 'oil = hen hole = hen house)

The Regional Commissioner, Sir William Bartholomew, was visiting Water Street, Hinchliffe Mill just after the flood. He spoke to Miss Edith Beaumont about her experiences, when the flood burst in to her living room and forced her upstairs to her bedroom. She told the Commissioner that she had then gone downstairs again for her cat. Sir William could not believe that he had heard correctly. "You turned back for what?" he asked. "My cat", Edith replied. Sir William could not but marvel at the courage and good humour that he found.

Margaret Drake, a little girl of six, remembers vividly being astonished by a sight on the riverside near the Victoria Inn. A toilet, washed a startling white, stood upright in a sea of brown mud. It had been in the wooden toilet hut at the tennis club, but the whole structure had been washed away, leaving the toilet apparently poised for action. Margaret could not understand why it had been left there, nor why her father seemed to be more concerned with the dull piles of debris and damaged pipework.

Later, Margaret was very relieved that a kitten, for which she had been worrying her mother for days, had survived the flood in the Elephant and Castle pub. The kitten family had been resting on the settee as the flood water burst into the pub, and they had floated on the settee from one room into the hall. When the waters subsided, the kittens were deposited gently back to ground, a little shaken, maybe, but not stirred. The kitten was named Monty, after the British General, but sprang the final surprise by having kittens of her own.

Les Heywood found that the flood brought some pleasant if unexpected benefits. He was looking through the letter box of Alderson's café at Holmbridge and saw a kitten on a settee, sad, saturated and surprised, but alive. Later on, he and some friends found that some jars of sweets had been washed from the café and landed near his home. Naturally the jars were returned later, somewhat enlightened.

There were also stories which reinforce the dour, mean Yorkshire image.

One policeman was on duty keeping sightseers away from wrecked and dangerous buildings, when two women pushed past him to gaze at the devastation.

> *"Move on there"* said the Policeman.
> *"Give us a chance"* said one of the women. *"We have come all the way from Golcar to have a look."*
> *"Aye"* said the Policeman *"and I have come all the way from Marsden to keep you away."*

Two women (surely not the same ones) got off the bus and asked a passer-by the way to the flood.

> *"Go that way"* they were told, *"down Victoria Street, and you will see the damage at the bottom."*
> *"But we don't want to see the damage"* they said, *"We want to see the flood."*

A man alighted from the Barnsley bus to view the damage in Holmfirth, and someone rattled a collection box, for the flood fund, under his nose.

> *"Nay"* said the man *"I haven't seen owt yet."*

Thongsbridge Cricket ground and bowling green were completely covered with about 150 tons of sludge, stones and debris. A laconic notice on the Bowling Club house door stated "No bowling allowed on Whit Tuesday."

A few days after the flood a loudspeaker van visited the village of Holme, 1000 feet up Holme Moss, and announced that the Huddersfield Corporation gas main had been mended and that anybody not getting a proper supply must inform the authorities. It overlooked the fact that the village had not had a gas supply for about 50 years.

SUMMARY OF THOSE DROWNED IN THE GREAT FLOOD, 1852

Family Name	Adults (with Ages)		Children (12 and over) Ages		Children (under 12) Ages		TOTAL DEAD
HINCHLIFFE MILL - FOLD GATE							5
Booth	James	60					
	Nancy	44					
Heeley	William	45					
Brook	Lydia	29			Hannah	10	
HINCHLIFFE MILL - WATER STREET							35
Marsden	Nancy	53	Joe	18			
	Eliza	46	Joshua	16			
Dodd	Joseph	48			Elizabeth	7	
	Hannah	30			Sarah Hannah	1	
Crosland	Jonathan	39	Mary	19	Foster	7	
	Joshua	21	Hannah	17	Ralph	3	
			Martha	15			
			Charles	13			
Charlesworth	Rose	39	Joshua	16	Hamor	6	
			James	14	John	4	
					Ruth	1	
Mettrick	James	58			Alfred	8	
	Mary	37			Jane	4	
	William	31			Joe	1	
	Samuel	21					
Earnshaw	Joshua	72	Ann (Beaumont)	13	Abel	6	
	Charles	36					
	Betty	26					
Exley	William	31					
VICTORIA - DYSON'S MILL							4
Sandford	Jonathan	45			Sarah Jane	9	
					Emily	4	
Wood	Ellen	22					
HOLMFIRTH - SCARFOLD							11
Woodcock			Alfred	17			
			Sarah	12			
Hellawell	Mary	28			George	9	
					Sarah	6	
					Elizabeth	4	
					John	2	
					Ann	9 months	
Bailey	Hannah	30			Ann	4	
					Martha	1	
HOLMFIRTH - HOLLOWGATE							10
Greenwood	Samuel	46					
	Lydia	45					
Matthews			Eliza	12			
Ashall	John	32			Alfred	2	
	Margaret	30					
Fearnes	Amelia	23			Lydia Ann	6 mths	
Thorpe					Charles	3	
Lee	James	65					
HOLMFIRTH - MILL HILL							12
Hartley	Sidney	41	Martha	16	Elizabeth	4	
	Mary Ann	39	James	14	Ellen Ann	2	
					George	10 weeks	
Shackleton	Richard	31			Hannah	8	
	Tamer	33			Grace Hirst	4	
					James	1	
SMITHY PLACE - BROCKHOLES							1
Heeley					Elizabeth	8	
							78
Plus three not named							3

TOTAL LOST IN THE FLOOD   81

APPENDIX 2

THE HOLMFIRTH MUSE

The Great Flood of 1852 was the inspiration for many sermons trying to explain the Divine Purpose in the tragedy which had so overwhelmed the Holme Valley. Similarly, many local poets were inspired to write of the tragic events in suitable Victorian style. Most are too long to print out in full, but a few verses will give a flavour of the deep feelings which were stirred up.

B Stanley from Cinderhill wrote nine verses 'Lines on the Great Flood at Holmfirth' as early as February, 1852, whilst the events were still fresh and vivid in his mind. Just a couple of verses will record his distress:

> Its onward sweep spared not the coffined dead,
> These scattered tombs bear witness of its power;
> While chapless skulls, torn from their silent bed,
> Darkened the gloom of that appalling hour.

> The aged, young, rich, poor, securely slept,
> Nor heard the deep howl of the frightful flood,
> Till like a demon o'er their homes it swept,
> And left but ruin where in peace they stood.

One poet, who wished to remain anonymous, wrote his "Lines on the Holmfirth Flood, occasioned by the Bursting of the Bilberry Dam, February 5, 1852, By which melancholy catastrophe 84 lives were Sacrificed" and had them published by Wm Rose of Sheffield. He concludes:

> Contemplate! - What an awful night!
> From life to death was tost.
> Each father mother child! engulphed,
> In raging billows lost!

> Oh! What a sad, heart-rending sight
> To morning's light was shewn
> Where cots, where mills, and mansions stood,
> Pale Death his wrecks had strewn!

> Prepare! Prepare! this loudly calls
> To each and all around
> Oft, as a thief, Death steals man's life
> 'Tis well if Heaven is found!

In 1909 George Wadsworth had set the words of a ballad by Joe Perkin to music, with four flats in six:eight time. Again, one verse of 'The Holmfirth Flood', to be sung as a solo, with sympathy, should suffice:

> It hurried along the weak and the strong,
> And crushed all around in its power;
> It rushed down the hill, took village and mill,
> The garden, the cottage and bower.
> It rolled through the glen, hurried women and men,
> Whilst peaceful and happy in slumber;
> It wrecked up the dead from their cold, cheerless bed,
> And its victims were lost in great number.

Some local authors went to the trouble of having their verse immortalised in print. Jonathan Hey only wrote 20 verses entitled 'Lines on the late Holmfirth Catastrophe' and had it printed to be framed, along with the tribute of the names and ages of all the deceased. He wrote as a Victorian poet and sounds like a Local Preacher, as he finishes with suitable prayers for the occasion.

> The silent dead, who long had slept,
> Yet still to friends and memory dear,
> Were from their peaceful harbour swept,
> And driven in its mad career.
> ....
> That when the flood of death shall come
> To sweep us from the earth away,
> We may obtain a brighter home,
> And live with thee in endless day.
>
> There we shall meet our friends again,
> Who on that night obtained their rest,
> And on Heaven's bright and sinless plain,
> With them in Christ be ever blest.

Charles Robinson wrote a small booklet containing two lengthy works; A Poem on those that were drowned (93 verses) and Poetry on the Bursting of the Bilberry Reservoir (83 verses). It was first published in 1854 and must have been quite successful as it ran to at least five editions, the latest in 1907, 55 years later. He must have spent a lot of time perusing the details of the flood for him to recount them in verse. His version of the rescue of James Mettrick is worth repeating:

> With the sincere the Lord is ever found,
> For his good providence doth gird the world around.
> Young Mettrick stands first upon the list,
> Whom God preserv'd, for death's sharp arrows miss'd.

When he arose, the house was tumbling down,
He with his bed into the flood was thrown;
And now commenced a most tremendous strife,
Nature, with all her powers, fought for life.

While struggling in the flood he felt despair,
But up he leap'd to taste the precious air,
And as he leap'd he caught a floating plank,
Which could not bear his weight, so down he sank.

Now every sinew took an active part,
He rolled and felt death near unto his heart;
Once more he leap'd, and caught a block of wood,
Which kept his head above the raging flood.

He now commenced a most amazing ride,
Death and destruction floated by his side;
By God's great mercy he did keep his hold,
While deadly things around his head were hurl'd.

Down into Bottom's dam he now doth launch,
The infidel may say 'tis all a chance;
But providence still guides his floating raft,
And screens his head from every deadly shaft.

Away he sail'd until he felt the sand,
When off he leap'd and soon escaped to land.
Thy relatives, alas! were swept away,
And Water Street in wreck and ruin lay.

APPENDIX 3

SCHEDULE OF FLOOD DAMAGE - 1944

The Holmfirth Urban District Council were involved in much of the operations to clear up the damage left by the flood in 1944. By 9th June Sidney G Dilnot, Clerk to the Council, had prepared an interim report on the flood, with the promise that in due course a complete report would be issued. Separately a report was issued in connection with all matters relating to food supplies. He listed the damage caused by the flood.

Industrial Premises

The number of industrial premises affected is 21, of which 13 are mills connected with the textile industry.

W.H. & J.Barber Ltd., Clarence Mill, Holmbridge. Concrete floors dislodged and portion of mill flooded. Goit and sewage disposal plant destroyed.

Whiteley & Green Ltd., Hinchliffe Mill. Extensive damage to finishing shed, part of which was flooded and silted up with mud and debris.

T. & J.Tinker Ltd., Bottoms Mill Foundations of mill adjoining river affected. Offices and shed flooded.

R.H.Dark & Co.Ltd., Riverside Mills. Half of sheds totally destroyed and contents consisting of bales swept into the river. Ground floor of mill flooded.

W.H.Battye & Sons,Ltd., Victoria Iron Works. The whole of the mill, consisting of two floors, flooded. Both floors covered with sludge to a depth of about 5ft.

W.Greenwood & Sons, Perseverance Mills. Flooded.

Wright Hinchliffe & Co.Ltd., Valley Dyeworks. Whole of premises flooded and covered with sludge.

H. & S. Butterworth Ltd., Lower Mill. Whole of mill flooded. Portion of mill collapsed owing to flooding. Extensive damage caused.

B.Mellor & Son, Ltd.,   Albert Mill.
Flooded.

J. & J.W.Longbottom,   Bridge Foundries.
Flooded.

R.L.Robinson,   Thongsbridge Mill.
Lower storey of mill flooded. Considerable debris and
sludge.

John Woodhead Ltd.,   Albion Mills,   Thongsbridge.
Flooded and bridge destroyed. Considerable debris and
sludge.

Boothroyd Rugs Ltd.,   Thongsbridge Mills.
Flooded.

J. Lancaster & Sons,Ltd.,   Lower Mytholmbridge Mills.
Very extensive damage by flooding and sludge. Damage to
weaving shed buildings.

J.Sykes & Co.,   Rock Mills,   Brockholes.
Very extensive damage by flooding and sludge. Portions
of new machinery lost.

Kaye   and   Messenger   Ltd.,   Candleworks,   Neiley,
Brockholes.
Flooded.   Shed collapsed.

G.W.Castle Ltd.,   Garage,   Holmfirth.
Baddeley Bros.Ltd. Garage,   Holmfirth.
Flooded. Damage to buildings.   Number of cars swept
away.

Allen Thornton & Co.Ltd.,   Crossley Mills,   Honley.
John Mitchell,   Brockholes.
Cooper Liversedge and Wood, Neiley Dyeworks, Honley.
A.C.Wickman Ltd.,   Reins Mill,   Honley

Flooded Shops

Approximately 60 shops affected, ranging from total
destruction to complete or partial immersion and sludging.
In many cases large quantities of stock have been totally or
partially destroyed, but in some cases the damage is
confined to cellars only.

In Victoria Street on the southern side were the premises of the Yorkshire Penny Bank Ltd. (with Prudential Assurance Co.Ltd. offices over), Messrs Wallaces, Grocers (dwelling house over), Mrs. Torr, milliner, and the Huddersfield Building Society. All these premises were built over the river and all of them collapsed into it. The first building to go was that of Messrs Wallaces, which collapsed into the river in two seconds, the whole of the building disappearing. The Yorkshire Penny Bank went next, but this subsided into the river much slower. The third building to go was that of the Huddersfield Building Society which, after shifting six inches from the premises of Messrs Gledhill and Brook, also subsided into the river and was totally immersed in less than two seconds.

Houses

In all, 109 houses were affected. The areas in which these houses were situated were:-

    Waterside and Ford Gate
    Hinchliffe Mill
    Water Street
    Scar Fold, Holmfirth
    Hollowgate
    Battye's Yard, Victoria
    Town Gate
    Foundry Yard
    Norridge Bottom
    Rock Terrace, Brockholes

River bed and banks

The whole of the river bed from Bilberry to Honley is very seriously affected. Approximately half of the river walls are washed away. In many cases the river has been diverted from its original course either on one bank or the other, and an additional feature has been the silting up of the original river bed in some cases as much as 4' either on one side or the other with consequent erosion on the other side. The agricultural land north of Bottoms Mill is covered with rocks (weighing as much as one ton) and debris over an area of 2 1/2 acres. The position is complicated by reason of the fact that the main sewer for the district is laid in the river from Holmbridge to Neiley, Brockholes. One of the major difficulties to be faced is restoring the river to its original channel and confining it to such channel.

Bridges

The whole of the bridges from Bilberry to Honley, with the exception of those at Bridge Lane and Smithy Place, have had their parapets swept away. There are also two other exceptions   the concrete bridges across the river in Hollowgate to Messrs. Castle's and Baddeley's Garages.

It has been mentioned earlier in this report the effect caused by the collapse of some of these parapet walls. Although the arches of the bridges appear to be untouched, it is feared that the arch of the bridge in Victoria Street is affected. A detailed examination will have to be made of each of the bridges to ensure that they are quite safe.

THE SUMMER WINE CONNECTION

The long running comedy series "Last of the Summer Wine" brought new life and interest to the town of Holmfirth and a wide area around. The scenes of the activities of Foggy, Compo and Clegg have made the area so well known that tourists come by the busload to see where it all happened.

The comedy trio, to say nothing of Blamire, Seymour, Truly and their other comic associates, were not present at the flood; they should all have been on active service during the hostilities. The brief series "First of the Summer Wine" was set before the war, so we can reliably surmise what would have happened if they had been in place during the flood in 1944.

At Hinchliffe Mill Wesley and Edie Pegden would have just been a few inches above the flood, situated as they were some thirty yards from the river. Their garage would have been well above the flood water, but they could have observed the flood rise up the walls of the Ford Gate houses, and sweep away Mrs Greensmith's riverside toilet. They would have seen debris carried along by the torrent and the walls alongside the river collapse. Later they would have seen the carpets strung out across the river to dry out.

On the approach to Holmfirth at Upperbridge, Compo would have had to retreat up to his bedroom in his Scarfold home as the lower floor was flooded. Then he would have achieved an ambition which, we are constantly told, he has harboured for years. The ceiling of his house would have to be opened up and he would have to be hauled up into the home of Nora Batty! Clearly, truth is stranger than fiction!

Clegg would have been high above the river, in his former home looking over the Church tower. His neighbours, Howard and Pearl, could have joined him with a similar bird's eye view of the devastation caused by the flood in the town centre.

Sid and Ivy, in their cafe in the small square alongside the Church, would have just avoided being flooded, but it would have seemed to be touch and go for a time. The waters swept along the road only ten metres away and Mrs Schofield, in 1944, drowned not far away. Sid and Ivy would no doubt have been in the forefront of providing help and succour, in the form of tea and sticky buns, to the helpers and rescuers who came to clear up the mess.

Blamire, Foggy, Seymour and Truly would have been well away from the flood in their respective houses and in the pubs which they all patronise. The Summer Wine characters are not seen in the town centre pubs - perhaps the landlords have very sensibly banned them.

'Last of the Summer Wine' is the longest running TV situation comedy in the world, and fact and fiction are becoming strangely entwined. The characters have blended in so well with the Holmfirth folk that they are part of the actual as well as the fictitious situation. Bill Owen, playing the part of 'Compo' Simonite, was so at home in Holmfirth that it became his second home. Sadly, he died whilst a series was being filmed and he was buried at Upperthong Church in 1999.

The storyline had to be hastily rewritten so that Compo's funeral became a moving part of the show; a real life as well as a fictional tribute. Even more poignant was the fact that Bill was reunited with his son Tom, a situation that was mirrored in the show itself. Tom now carries on the family tradition, although with his own character.

Compo's tombstone in the Churchyard at Upperthong overlooks the centre of Holmfirth, as he wished. It is engraved 'Here lies Wm J Owen Rowbotham, Actor, Playright' and nearby is a replica pair of his trademark wellies. Plans are also in hand for a statue of the rascal to be erected on Huddersfield Road, almost opposite Upperbridge. It will be just near enough for Nora Batty, with her yard brush, to keep her eye on him from a safe distance.

APPENDIX 5

GETTING A GRIP ON WATER

The accounts of the floods in both 1852 and 1944, taken from the original records, report all the details in the old imperial measurements - yards, feet and gallons.

Younger readers may be confused by these old English measurements, so the following metric equivalents might be useful:

Twelve inches equals one foot
One inch equals 25 millimetres (mm), or 2.5 centimetres (cm)
One foot equals 300 mm, or 30 cm
Three feet equal one yard
One metre (m) equals one yard and 3.4 inches, or about 1.1 yards
In simpler terms, 10 feet approximately equals 3 metres
One kilometer is 1000 metres, about five eights of a mile

An acre is a measure of land area and is 4840 square yards
There are 640 acres in a square mile
There are about 250 acres in a square kilometer

It is an oddity of the old Imperial measurements that the vertical scale is usually quoted in feet, and the horizontal scale in yards and miles. So a mountain may be 1800 feet high, not 600 yards, and never one third of a mile. On the other hand, a building will be 100 yards away, not 300 feet; although very short distances may be quoted in feet. There is no similar distinction in Metric measurements.

Water Volumes

It is difficult to grasp water in quantity, whether in gallons or litres. All the floods mentioned in this book involved considerable quantities of water. It has been estimated that the cloudburst in 1944 produced three to four inches of rain in an hour and a half. This is a lot of rain - but how much?

Put another way, four inches of rain (or 10 centimetres, in metric) would produce about 411 cubic metres of water per acre. One cubic metre of water weighs a ton, so we have 411 tons of rain per acre, or 260,000 tons per square mile.

Looked at another way, a cubic metre of water is 1000 litres, or 220 gallons. This provides over 90,000 gallons of water per acre, or 58 million gallons of water per square mile.

Either way, this tremendous amount of water, decanted into a narrow valley, was more than sufficient to cause the widespread destruction described. Water in this quantity, and moving at such a pace, has a force to carry everything before it.

IAN HARLOW - BIOGRAPHICAL NOTES

Ian Harlow is an exiled Yorkshireman, living in Nottingham but having a little cottage in Holmfirth. During the war he was doubly fortunate to be evacuated from Hull to Hinchliffe Mill to stay with an Uncle and Aunt, before the family procured a cottage to rent for the duration of hostilities. Doubly fortunate, since Holmfirth proved to be (for a youngster) a very peaceful and happy place; whereas the family home in Hull was destroyed by enemy action.

He was in Holmfirth at the time of the 1944 flood and the memories of that occasion are still vivid. Although the flood was overlooked because of the momentous events taking place elsewhere in Europe, everybody concerned in Holmfirth had a story to tell and many of these are recounted in this book.

After the war the family returned to Hull. Ian later married Mary and they had two children, Alison and Charles. He is now retired, but worked as an accountant spending four years in Zambia before resuming his career in England. The family lived in Devon for a short time before moving to Nottingham where he worked in the textile industry and later British Telecom.